INDIE AUTHOR MAGAZINE

HELLO AND WELCOME!

I'm Indie Annie, and I'm thrilled you're reading this gorgeous full-color version of IAM. Did you know that you can also access all the information, education, and inspiration in our app? It's available on both the iOS App Store and Google Play. And for those that prefer to listen to me read articles, you can pop over to Spotify or our website. Happy Reading!

X

IndieAuthorMagazine.com

Download on the **App Store**

GET IT ON **Google Play**

Spotify

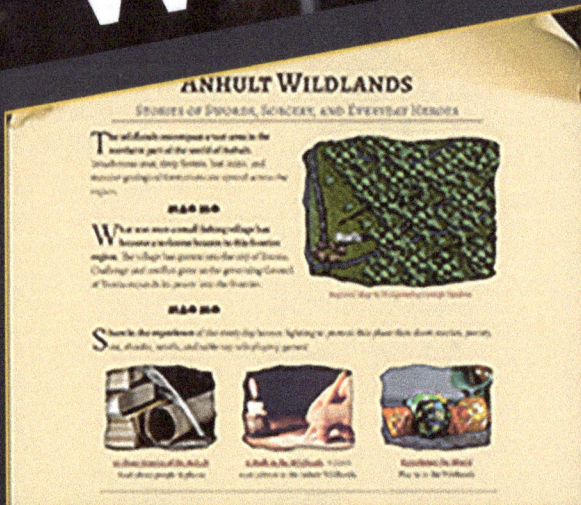

OUTLINING

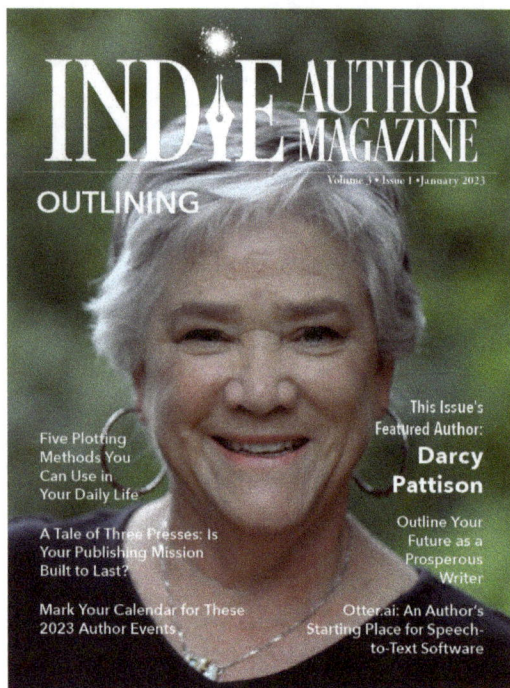

ON THE COVER

REGULAR COLUMNS

THE WRITE LIFE

TYPEWRITER TALES

INDiE
AUTHOR MAGAZINE

EDITORIAL

Publisher | Chelle Honiker

Editor in Chief | Nicole Schroeder

Creative Director | Alice Briggs

Copy Editor | Lisa Thompson

ADVERTISING & MARKETING

Inquiries | Jorge Mata
advertising@IndieAuthorMagazine.com

Information
https://IndieAuthorMagazine.com/
advertising/

CONTRIBUTORS

Angela Archer, Elaine Bateman, Maureen Bonatch, Patricia Carr, Bradley Charbonneau, Honorée Corder, Jackie Dana, Heather Clement Davis, Jamie Davis, Laurel Decher, Fatima Fayez, Gill Fernley, Greg Fishbone, Belinda Griffin, Jac Harmon, Audrey Hughey, Marion Hermannsen, Chrishaun Keller-Hanna, Kasia Lasinska, Monica Leonelle, Jenn Lessman, Megan Linski-Fox, Craig Martelle, Angie Martin, Kevin McLaughlin, Lasairiona McMaster, Jenn Mitchell, Susan Odev, Eryka Parker, Clare Sager, Robyn Sarty, Joe Solari, Gayle Trent, Terry Wells-Brown

SUBSCRIPTIONS
https://indieauthormagazine.com/subscribe/

HOW TO READ
https://indieauthormagazine.com/how-to-read/

WHEN WRITING MEANS BUSINESS
IndieAuthorMagazine.com

Athenia Creative | 6820 Apus Dr., Sparks, NV, 89436 USA | 775.298.1925

ISSN 2768-7880 (online)–ISSN 2768-7872 (print)

Design like a Pro for free

👑 Try Canva Pro today

Canva

https://writelink.to/canva

FROM THE PUBLISHER

THE SECRET TO SUSTAINING NEW YEAR'S RESOLUTIONS: VALUES-BASED ALIGNMENT

After years of failing to keep my New Year's resolutions, I gave up.

But that's not to say that I gave up on making life changes.

I stopped with the grand declarations followed by the inevitable failure, and instead, I thought about the reasons those changes were significant to me. Those underlying reasons became a core set of values designed to drive every decision I made on a day-to-day basis.

I adopted a philosophy of aligning my decisions—all my choices—to some core values, defined as beliefs I hold sacred.

First, I thought about what I wanted my life to look like if there weren't a single obstacle in my way. What would bring me peace and joy? I journaled. I asked myself hard questions and had to think about the answers. For example, "Is it good for me to want to be rich? Or is that selfish when there's so much suffering in the world?" I won't bore you with my philosophical and existential crises. I will say that following that period of contemplation, I distilled all that angst down to a core set of personal values that look like this:

I want to be

- financially peaceful
- creatively free
- light in obligations
- politically active
- image confident
- ready for adventure

I've published a deeper dive on Medium about what those mean, but I can assure you, it's been a game changer. I no longer feel like I've failed on February 1, and that feels like an accomplishment.

From the entire team at *Indie Author Magazine*, we hope that 2023 will be your most creative and prosperous year ever.

To Your Success,
Chelle
Publisher
Indie Author Magazine

FROM THE EDITOR IN CHIEF

I have an honest confession to make: I've been staring at my computer for a few minutes now, trying to figure out what I want this letter to say.

I've fallen victim to the Curse of the Blank Page plenty of times. When editing is part of your day job, it makes it difficult to turn off your inner critic and get words down. Or maybe that's just the excuse I use to sneak the red pen into my own first drafts. Having an outline helps—I'm a plotter, through and through—but it's not always the perfect answer either. Suffice it to say, as I think about how to start this first letter in the first issue of a new year, I'm not surprised to be staring at a blinking cursor.

Perhaps you've had the same feeling recently. The beginning of a new year is a blank page all its own, filled with so much possibility that it can almost become overwhelming. Projects and events already marked on your calendar. Others you're hoping will be soon. Still more that you likely haven't even considered yet. But there's something I think we often miss, both as authors and as people, when we're looking ahead at all these unknowns: There's beauty in a blank page.

That white space, whether it's the start of a manuscript or the first page in your planner, is infinitely larger than the space it takes up on your desk. But you won't have to fill it all at once. You can start with a goal, the same way Marti Dumas' career in publishing began with her dream of gifting her son a book. You can start with an outline—and if plotting helps you feel more prepared at the start of a new story, why not try those same methods to organize your author business too? You can start with a single letter, and before you know it, those letters will fill the page.

All that matters is that you start.

Nicole Schroeder
Editor in Chief
Indie Author Magazine

The Rising Tide

This past month, more than eighteen hundred independent authors gathered at Bally's Event Center in Las Vegas, Nevada, to learn, to grow, and to celebrate their work as publishing professionals. We welcomed them with messages of inspiration and advice for finding success, however you define it. This month, I want to offer that same welcome to you all.

· ❧ · ❧ · ❧ ·

This is Michael Anderle and I'm Craig Martelle. Welcome to 20Books Vegas.

Welcome to the greatest gathering of independent authors in the world. Look across the sea of people—single drops that create an ocean and a rising tide.

We have doctors and lawyers, retirees, people slaving away at a soul-sucking day job, and even students, still learning what life is all about. A wealth of experience and knowledge is right here, along with the wealth of imagination. The greatness that exists within your minds and the perseverance to put those thoughts on paper and then publish those words, baring your soul before the world.

This reminds me of a quote by Teddy Roosevelt, which is applicable to all.

"It is not the critic who counts; not the man who points out how the strong man stumbles, or where the doer of deeds could have done them better. The credit belongs to the man who is actually in the arena, whose face is marred by dust and sweat and blood; who strives valiantly; who errs, who comes short again and again, because there is no effort without error and shortcoming; but who does actually strive to do the deeds; who knows great enthusiasms, the great devotions; who spends himself in a worthy cause; who at the best knows in the end the triumph of high achievement, and who at the worst, if he fails, at least fails while daring greatly, so that his place shall never be with those cold and timid souls who neither know victory nor defeat."

The critics don't matter. Only the readers, those people who vote with their money. They are forgiving if you've told a great story, and why wouldn't it be great? It was great in your mind and great enough that you committed a month of your life, or a year, to get that story down. It was great then. It should be great now.

Whether your imagination or the words you used to portray what you've seen in your mind, all of it can get better with practice. Explore within. Shape the words. And then do it again. Practice is the palette before your easel. I won't stand up here and tell you that any of it is easy. It's hard. There's no passive income with being a writer. You have to work at it. As John F. Kennedy said, who, by the way, was the originator of the rising tide quote, "We do this not because it is easy but because it is hard."

Working hard at the right things can deliver a pot of gold at the end of the rainbow, but isn't the journey through the sunshine worth it? It takes the rain before you can see the rainbow, but it takes the sun to show you how vast the world can be through the prism of the rain. Like the prism of your words.

The world will turn whether you turn with it or not. Life moves on, and those who are staying engaged and building a readership for their current books as well as their future books will be the ones who get to slow down and see what the world has to offer.

Success is a harsh taskmaster. You'll be enticed to push harder and harder. Only you know when you've pushed too hard.

Balance for those at the top. Balance for those breaking in.

But always remember why you wanted to write that story. Why did you want to educate unknown people? Because it's a calling. It's not a get-rich-quick scheme.

Carl Sagan said, "What an astonishing thing a book is. It's a flat object made from a tree with flexible parts on which are imprinted lots of funny dark squiggles. But one glance at it and you're inside the mind of another person, maybe somebody dead for thousands of years. Across the millennia, an author is speaking clearly and silently inside your head, directly to you. Writing is perhaps the greatest of human inventions, binding together people who never knew each other, citizens of distant epochs. Books break the shackles of time. A book is proof that humans are capable of working magic."

Seven short years ago, Michael Anderle and I wrote our first books. If anyone wonders, look what can be accomplished in seven short years. Millions of dollars earned selling fiction while also changing the entire industry by showing authors what's possible, showing people who want to be authors what's possible.

When the end is only the beginning, whole new vistas can open before you. After you've finished your book, then the real work starts, but there is nothing like seeing kind words from a stranger about your story, about your nonfiction. How it helped them through a tough time by taking their mind off their own problems or helping them fix their problems. There is nothing like giving people an escape or educating people with the power of your words.

Did you know what you were capable of? Have you already written your best story? I say you haven't because there's always the opportunity to do a little better, be a little different. Find a new audience. Why do old golfers keep playing even though they can't hit the ball as far and can't walk as fast? It's the joy of the challenge.

No matter where we are on our journey, we can always look forward. No one has ever reached a peak and said, "There is nowhere left to climb." No one. The climb isn't about finishing. It's about looking back to see how far you've come, from an empty page to a chapter to a completed story—to strangers reading it. And starting all over again, but though the page is blank, you're not starting fresh. You have learned through the words you have massaged before.

Like a seasoned carpenter shapes wood and bends it to their will, a wordsmith weaves the words to build a prism that translates the images from an author's mind to the mind of the reader, drawing them into the artistry and majesty of the world that you created.

Let's get to the business at hand: 20Books Vegas. Look at the craft sessions. Look at the business or the genre or deeper aspects of publishing, like alternate revenue streams. All of the vendors and industry professionals are here to answer your questions.

The 20Books shows have been described as "life changing." That's your investment in yourself because you saw what was possible. Then you grabbed it and held on, refusing to quit through the hard days, half blind from staring at your screen, from a marathon writing session to often conflicting marketing and promotional ideas when you've run out of money before you've made any. But you persevere because it's the only way forward. Stopping isn't what you   started for.

All failure begins with the expectation of success, but failure isn't final. It's only a stepping stone to get better. To be better. To join the ranks of those making good money being an author.

Success is a mountain that we all climb in our own way, higher and higher. We've found that it's easier going when we reach a hand back to help someone else.

Because writing is a lonely business, and that's okay, but sometimes, it's better to be alone together.

Sharpen your eyeballs, and brace your ears. All of our speakers are well established in their genres and in the industry. Watch and listen, and if you can, talk to people because someone here will say something that will truly change your life. You have only to hear it. And who knows, something you say could make a difference too. We're at different stages in our journeys. And we're all here for the chance to improve our business—the business of being an author and a publisher.

Be the change you need in your life. Be a part of the rising tide. ■

Craig Martelle

Dear Indie Annie,

I am desperate to fulfill my dream of being a published writer. It's all I've ever wanted since I was a child, which I am embarrassed to say was over five decades ago. Is it too late? Have I missed the boat? I don't even know where to start!

Clueless in Calgary

DEAR CLUELESS,

Oh boy, doesn't it suck getting old? Seeing all your youthful dreams slip through your gnarly fingers? Watching your peers climb up the ladders of their chosen careers whilst you make do with whatever it is you are making do with?

You don't say if you are working in a writing-adjacent role. You know, the occupations that use your mastery of words and imaginative ideas in some other guise. Perhaps you are a teacher or a journalist, a lawyer or a marketing executive. Or maybe you have been happy working in the cheese section at your local supermarket.

To be honest, my dear Clueless, it matters not a jot. Your past does not dictate your future. For example, it would amaze you how many successful authors have been in the military or were stay-at-home moms.

If the past five decades have helped you to refine your prose, that's wonderful. Perhaps you haven't written a word since high school and, my dear, that is also wonderful. Whatever has happened, it has brought you to this moment. Right here. Right now.

I once attended a writing conference—a small, local affair, where a literary agent was holding court from the stage to a room full of wannabe authors. Beside her sat a mature lady, I would hazard somewhere in her early sixties, talking about securing her first six-figure publishing deal.

The audience wanted to know how many rejection letters she had received. How many unpublished manuscripts lay gathering dust on her shelves? Most of those present wanted to gauge how much pain and suffering they collectively shared with the now-successful author before them. They

needed her to throw them crumbs of hope to mop up their despair.

They received none.

This was her first book.

She wrote it as a bet during National Novel Writing Month (NaNoWriMo) the previous November.

The mood in the room changed. Then, a creative writing lecturer from a nearby university stood up and asked the literary agent a different question.

"I have been writing and teaching the art of writing for twenty years. I have sent off hundreds of manuscripts, and all have been rejected. Tell me, what do I need to do to get you to take on one of my books?"

The agent took the microphone and replied, "Write something people want to read."

When pushed further, her continued advice was, "Write something I can sell."

You see, dear Clueless, your future readers don't care if you hold a PhD in creative writing, have spent all your adult life studying the occult in Historical Romance literature, or once worked at *The Washington Post* or the local post office. They want a good book.

So where do you start? Perhaps, like my friend on that stage, you could join NaNoWriMo. Maybe there is a local writers' group near you? There are also plenty of useful books and online courses that could help you with plot structure, world and character building, or how to self-publish. Why, my sweet, even this humble magazine has more than enough information to get up to speed on what to do next.

My best advice to you is to just start. Pick an idea and begin. You can plot or pants your way through a draft, whatever works for you. You can learn to self-edit or hire a professional. You can seek out literary agents or publish yourself. The important thing is that you stop telling yourself you are too old and instead celebrate that you have over fifty years of life to draw upon.

You have fifty glorious years of meeting, working with, hating, and loving other people. Fifty years of good and bad stuff happening to you and around you. Fifty years of ideas and inspiration. Fifty years of you.

It's never too late. Start today.

Happy writing,
Indie Annie

X

10 TIPS FOR

FIVERR

As authors, we know how valuable time is. However, this non-renewable resource tends to slip between our fingers when it comes to accomplishing tasks we lack either the time or expertise to complete. Outsourcing tasks by using a freelance network platform like Fiverr can help save you time and money and prevent you from spinning your wheels while trying to get your book to market. You can learn the difference between cheap labor and work from a professional that's of a great value and fits well within your budget.

WHAT IS FIVERR?

Fiverr is a global professional freelance marketplace that has been connecting sellers and buyers on a secure platform since 2010. Its name comes from the minimum starting price of five dollars initially set for services, or "gigs," offered on the site. Through Fiverr, you can find professionals offering services at affordable prices for anything from ghostwriting, illustrations, and web design to contracts and marketing services. When outsourcing tasks to small businesses and freelance creators, it's important to conduct extensive research and become as knowledgeable as possible about the process beforehand. This can help create an experience you can benefit from and revisit while navigating the publishing process. Fiverr's encrypted, secure platform protects both parties from fraudulent transactions, so any business conducted directly on the platform with new sellers is ensured to be a safe and smooth exchange.

Here are a few tips for setting proper expectations and preparing for the outsourcing process.

1 GET CLEAR ON WHAT YOU WANT

The first step for a successful experience on Fiverr is to plan. Spend some time thinking about why you're seeking assistance on your project or the service or product you need. Next, get as clear as possible about what your desired outcome will look like. Would you like a targeted social media ad, a carefully curated lead magnet, or a showstopping book cover? What problem will your ideal product solve? What is your budget, and what time frame works best for your needs? Knowing what you want will help you understand what to look for when selecting the best seller.

② USE A DETAILED SEARCH

The service headings on the Fiverr website are useful for finding the specific type of service you want. Take some time to navigate the wide range of services offered. If you don't see the exact service you want, or you're overwhelmed by the number of results, use short-tailed keywords to refine the results. For example, "education book reviewer" or "Historical Romance book reviewer" will provide more useful options than "book reviewer."

Pro Tip: You can also favorite the profiles of sellers you are interested in by clicking on the heart icon in the upper right-hand corner of their profile. Visit your favorites list from time to time to check their availability for upcoming projects or to see if they're running any promotions. By doing so, you may also receive email alerts for similar products and services.

③ BE MINDFUL OF THE SELLER'S NUMBER OF REVIEWERS AND AVERAGE RATING

Gauging how many customers a seller has worked with and their average ratings helps paint a quick picture of the type of experience you can expect while working with them. Fiverr uses levels to categorize their sellers based on monthly performance, the timeliness of the project completion, and buyer satisfaction. A Level 1 Seller with a fast response rate and an average rating above 4.5 is a viable option. A Level 2 Seller on Fiverr has completed at least fifty orders on time, with an average rating of 4.7 or higher.

Pro Tip: You can save money by working with a New Seller. These freelancers are often seeking the criteria to reach Level 1 Seller status and may be open to offering reasonable services to build their portfolio and favorable ratings. Be mindful that sellers must be active for at least sixty days and need to have met quantity and revenue criteria to be eligible for Level 1 Seller status. A quick look at a seller's full profile will show you how long they have been a member, their last project delivery, and any customer review details.

④ HEED FIVERR'S RECOMMENDATIONS

After you've spent time on the site, Fiverr will provide a list in their recommendation tab based on your search history. Be sure to check this section regularly to ensure you're weighing all of your options during your vetting process. The list often includes sellers with high customer rankings who have worked with several customers. If these things are important to you and time is of the essence, it may be a great option.

5 CONVERSE WITH MULTIPLE SELLERS

Reach out to sellers who meet your criteria to learn more about them. This can help you determine the best fit for your project. Ask specific questions to identify whether they possess your desired qualifications, have provided past results that match what you're looking for, and can meet your deadline. Remember to request proof of results in your specific niche. For example, if you're a self-help writer and they've only worked with Sci-Fi authors, determine whether they'll be able to provide the results you're looking for before moving forward.

6 REQUEST THE SELLER'S PORTFOLIO, AND STUDY SIMILAR CUSTOMER REVIEWS

When looking into a seller, be sure to review the quality and results of their past projects. If they have a tangible service, they should have a portfolio listed on their profile. If not, they will likely have a list of deliverables on their profile that tells you what to expect while working with them. Ensure the language on their profile is thorough, concise, and error-free. One of the best ways to determine the level of quality a seller can provide is to study their customers' experiences. Check the negative and positive reviews that pertain to your project. How did the customer say they were treated? Were their expectations met? Would they recommend the seller?

7 UNDERSTAND WHAT YOU'RE PAYING FOR AND WHAT YOU'LL RECEIVE UP FRONT

Depending on the type of service offered, sellers provide tiers of service for their customers ranging between basic, standard, and premium packages. Full payment for the service is required up front. If the terms of your desired service aren't included in the packages listed, you can contact the seller to request additional services. For example, if their standard graphic design package includes a 3-D mockup cover, but you don't need one, you can message the seller and request a replacement item or a price adjustment. Also, you'll want to negotiate the number of post-delivery revisions the seller is willing to make on the project before entering the agreement. Give yourself time to review and approve their work within three days of delivery. After that time period, Fiverr automatically marks projects as complete. After a project's completion, it will be the seller's decision whether to honor additional revision requests or to require a new project agreement for revisions or additional services.

Pro Tip: Payment options include credit card, PayPal, or Apple Pay. Fiverr uses the real-time EUR/USD exchange rate to calculate total costs in US dollars at checkout.

⑧ BE RESPONSIVE

Your seller will likely be in touch with you throughout the process. It's important to keep lines of communication open by being accessible to the seller in case they have questions about your project. Download the Fiverr app and turn on your notifications so that you're instantly aware of any efforts the seller makes to get in touch with you. This is especially important post-project delivery when you're in the three-day grace period.

Pro Tip: To help create a healthy working relationship for you and your seller, be cognizant of the seller's time zone and remember that they must also honor project deadlines for other clients.

⑨ OVERWHELMED? CREATE YOUR OWN GIG!

If you're drowning in viable seller options, no matter how refined your search results, you always have the option to create your own gig for a base fee of five dollars. This allows you to set a project price within your budget while freelancers bid on the opportunity to work with you. Benefits of creating a gig include:

- being in control of the process
- getting as detailed as necessary regarding the project details and your expectations
- drawing serious inquiries only
- avoiding the need to negotiate on price
- Setting a deadline that works for you

Just remember to provide necessary reference documents or websites, qualifications, and the appropriate timeline and process details to ensure a smooth transaction.

⑩ MIND YOUR P'S AND Q'S

If your project's quality weren't important to you, you wouldn't be open to hiring a freelancer. Etiquette is key when partnering with others on creating a project that will represent you in the best way possible. Be kind to your seller and cultivate a relationship with them that can result in repeat business. Having a reliable professional who is willing and able to support your mission is a beautiful thing, so treat your seller well, and they'll be happy to see your name in their inbox in the future. ■

Eryka Parker

M is for Mims House

CHILDREN'S AUTHOR-PUBLISHER DARCY PATTISON BUILDS HER BRAND WITH THE YOUNGEST READERS IN MIND

Ten years ago, children's author Darcy Pattison faced a dilemma. After publishing with multiple traditional publishers—Lothrup, Lee & Shepard; Harcourt Inc.; Sylvan Dell Publishers; Philomel; and Stone Arch Books—from 1991 to 2011, she couldn't find the right home for a nonfiction picture book about the oldest bird in the world. Publishers she approached wanted to make a book about the bird or about the people, but no one shared her vision for the book. So she decided to find a new way to bring this story to life and enticed an illustrator friend, Kitty Harvill, to collaborate by sending her "visual material" until she fell in love with the albatross too.

Then, they brought the book to market themselves.

After Pattison published *Wisdom: The Midway Albatross* in 2013, the book won a national award—first place in *Writer's Digest*'s 20th Annual Self-Published Book Awards—and earned a coveted starred review in *Publishers Weekly*. Recognized for years as a knowledgeable and generous author and writing teacher, Pattison became an award-winning publisher as well.

That decision would become just the first step on an entirely new path in Pattison's career. After taking WMG Publishing's Master Business Class (https://wmgworkshops.com) from Kristine Kathryn Rusch and Dean Wesley Smith on building a publishing business, Pattison bought a thousand ISBNs, a commitment that's carried her to where she is today. "It was a line in the sand," she says. "I'm going to do this, and I'm not going to look back."

Nearly a decade later, the hardworking owner of the publishing company Mims House (https://mimshousebooks.com) has followed up her earlier success with a National Council of Teachers of English Notable Children's

All photos by Dwight Pattison

Book Award in 2018; National Science Teaching Association Outstanding Science Trade Book awards in 2015, 2017, 2019, and 2020; and a Notable Social Studies Trade Book Award in 2021. Her award-winning books are popular with readers too. *A Little Bit of Dinosaur* reached one and a half million reads on the Epic! reading app, popular with schools and families.

Among indie authors, Pattison is well known for her ability to find new publishing opportunities. It's one of her many superpowers, as well as one that's helped her navigate the challenging world of children's publishing. "I really try for excellence," she says.

Instead of a rigid launch list, Pattison has an intuitive publishing style. She steps back periodically to review her extensive catalog and studies her successes, saying, "This is working. What else can I do?" She brings each new book to market in the best way for that book, but her publishing touchstones include:

- **Awareness:** The librarian listserv that she's been on for many years keeps her aware of the wider world of children's books. She's always looking for "places to listen," like newsletters for children's books from *Publishers Weekly*, the Children's Book Council, and the American Booksellers Association. To authors who are trying to find their own space in the genre, she says it's important to "take the time to learn what's out there already and how this compares, how to make a difference." It's the same list of questions she asked herself when she published that nonfiction picture book about Wisdom the Albatross, in order to understand the story's place in "the wider world of children's literature."

- **Discoverability:** Metadata is a publishing superpower, Pattison says, and she has a toolbox full of publishing tools to give her primary audience—schools and librarians—what they need: Lexile measures (https://meta-metricsinc.com/publisher-toolkit) to indicate each book's reading level, interest level, and grade level; cataloging-in-publication data, or CIP blocks, for librarians for the books' copyright pages; and respected awards and reviews.

- **Experiments:** Arnold Schwarzenegger alternated between *Terminator* and *Kindergarten Cop*. Pattison took a page out of his playbook and started alternating between children's Fantasy and children's nonfiction. Eventually,

she says, "the nonfiction took off." Her willingness to test new creative ideas is one of her hallmarks, maybe because of her strong commitment to the creative life. "I want a life that's artistic in this creative way, and traditional publishing didn't give me that. So if I can create that space for myself, that's why I'm here."

- **Advocacy:** When applying for editorial reviews, awards, or other opportunities, mindset can make the difference between success and not applying at all. "Don't disqualify yourself," Pattison says. A focus on excellence makes it much easier to advocate for the books. "Never apologize for your books," she says. Instead of referring to books as "self-published," she talks about "bringing a book to market." This puts the focus where it belongs: on the audience her book will serve.

- **Excellence:** Pattison advises authors to do more than "just put the book out there." Instead, she says, ask how your book can join the conversations already being had in your genre." The concept is a cornerstone for Mims House. Quality and marketing are baked right in, with three or four entry points into each book that add more value through connections to curricula, educational standards, or key concepts.

"I'm trying to build in multiple layers of why someone would need my book in their classroom," she says. "It doesn't always work, but I think that's one of my super strengths … [to take] an idea and then think of layers."

One of her traditionally published books, *Prairie Storms*, adds these layers in three parts. "I'm bringing in animals, then the weather, and then I organized it by month," she explains. "In the early classrooms, when they're learning the months of the year, they can use it for that, so there are three ways in. If I can get three ways into a book or four or five, then it's much more likely to sell." When Pattison is looking at a science idea, she looks at the science standards in the United States to see what is required at different age levels and what she might work into a story for her target age group. "I'm thinking about the idea," she says. "Can I do it by months? Can I add colors? Can I add numbers? … I'm thinking of all of those things as … I try to write a great story."

· ℰↃ · ℰↃ · ℰↃ ·

As a publisher, Pattison says, the books you choose to publish and how you approach topics or stories define your brand. For the library and school markets, these are key selling points. "Your reputation just builds over the years," Pattison says. "Now, when a science teacher gets a book from Mims House, they know that place—or I hope they do." It can start with something as small as the consistent use of markers like name, logo, fonts, or colors. For Mims House, it might be a "feel to the art"—a natural extension of Pattison's other creative outlets in quilting and collage work. It might also be readers' familiarity with the publisher's other titles. "Mims House has developed a reputation for really great science books for kids, and … hopefully for interesting novels for kids."

Despite her love of watercolors, collages, and color, Pattison doesn't do her own illustrations, but she's clearly an art director with a vision. "I've consistently used one illustrator, Peter Willis, from the UK, for eight or nine books now," she says. "He's fabulous. … He brings the fun, the playfulness, the colors, the composition, (and) all of that goes together and it creates this brand."

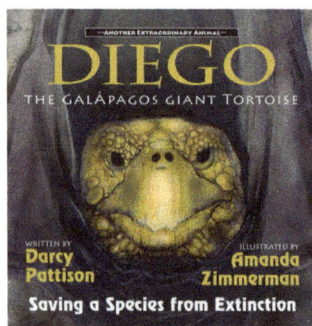

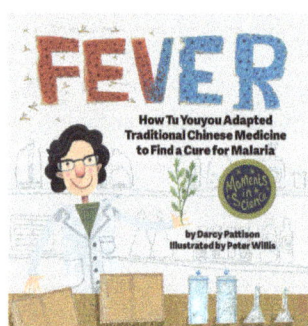

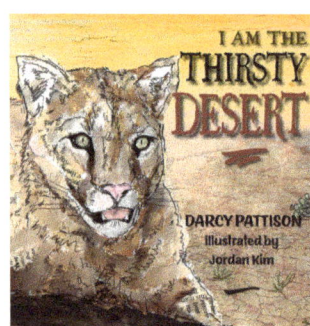

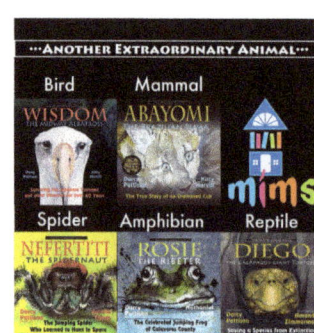

Still, Pattison's advanced color and composition skills aren't going to waste. Her quilting experience may deserve credit in a new project she's taken on with a traditional publisher, Dayspring, to design pop-ups for picture books based on traditional songs. Possibly most easily recognized as a greeting card manufacturer, Dayspring had no trouble making pop-ups or "paper engineering" that would be financially impossible for an indie publisher.

· ෆ · ෆ · ෆ ·

For Pattison, publishing is like writing fiction: There's a setup and a payoff. An established brand sets expectations that are fulfilled when your publishing delivers a quality product. "It's a different way of looking at it than, 'I'm just an author. I'm going to put my books out there,' she says." In the years she's spent writing her own books and publishing through Mims House, she's learned that bringing all her skills and experience into new opportunities is one of the best ways to quality books. "What would make someone look at a book and say, yes, that's a Mims House book? It's hard," Pattison says. "You have to allow your passions and your interests to come through. But if you can do that, then you can consistently build a collection that says this is a Mims House book."

Nine years after her first indie publishing success, Pattison's sixty-five titles have earned her numerous awards, starred reviews, and countless avid young readers. It was time to "translate that [interesting intellectual property] into something else for kids." In 2022, Pattison took her well-defined brand to a new level of creativity by exploring licensing at Kidscreen Summit 2022, Licensing Expo 2022, and a Women in Toys workshop. This past year, she also branched out into Kickstarter, boosting presales for her holiday picture book *The Plan for the Gingerbread House,* as well as for her Kittytuber series. With events like these, Pattison is actively listening to her target audiences, experimenting with new ways to add value, advocating for her books, and aiming for excellence.

The 2023 Mims House catalog showcases the consistent application of those same publishing touchstones that Pattison has used to drive her author career. Already, she's looking forward to her award-winning *Moments in Science* series coming out in Korean over the next year, and plenty more projects are in store for her young audience in the coming months. Keep an eye out for more publishing payoffs—after all, she still has eight hundred ISBNs left to go. ■

Laurel Decher

Viva 20Books Vegas!

EVERYTHING YOU MIGHT'VE MISSED AT THE 2022 CONFERENCE, FROM OFFICIAL EVENTS TO CONNECTIONS MADE AT THE CAKE MACHINE

Five days. Over fifty vendors. Nearly eighteen hundred in-person attendees, with even more tuning in virtually. By many accounts, the 20Books Vegas 2022 conference that took place November 14–18 at Bally's Events Center in—you guessed it—Las Vegas, Nevada, was one of the biggest to date. As the largest indie author conference of its kind, the event has drawn throngs of independent authors and others in the publishing industry together for years, giving them a place to connect with one another, grow their businesses, and celebrate the power of storytelling. And perhaps try a slice of vending machine cake.

Last year's five-day event kicked off Monday, November 14, with the second annual 20BooksTo50K® Vendor Day, bringing together more than fifty companies that serve the indie author

community. This event provided authors with an all-day opportunity to meet with representatives and learn more about the services that these companies offer. Some of the notable companies in attendance included Amazon, Blackstone Publishing, Podium Audio, Draft2Digital, and Google, each of which offers a wide range of services for indie authors, from publishing and distribution to marketing and promotion.

And the energy only ramped up from there. As with every year, the 2022 conference offered event-goers plenty of memorable moments. A group of students from Tennessee were able to explore the conference alongside the authors and other industry professionals in attendance. GameLit authors hosted Dungeons & Dragons sessions that took place over the course of the week. Authors took advantage of Tuesday's cosplay theme to dress up as favorite characters from popular franchises, as well as their own works. Attendees of Thursday's afternoon sessions saw some excitement when fire alarms—false alarms, it was determined—went off during a set of panels that included those for the Thriller and Post-Apocalyptic genres. And the Readers & Authors Vegas Event, or RAVE, brought readers into the mix Friday for the second year in a row. Event organizer Craig Martelle might've summed it up best in a Facebook post in the 20BooksTo50K® Facebook group following the event. "There was power in that audience," he wrote. "In one place and with positive attitudes that lifted the spirits of all."

Anyone who's attended a 20Books conference in years past will understand that even for those who made it to the 2022 event, it's impossible to have seen it all. That's why *IAM* has rounded up the most memorable parts and important lessons from every corner of 20Books Vegas 2022, from the sessions and events that were part of the official schedule to the networking opportunities authors found between the lines.

20BOOKS VEGAS, TWENTY THOUSAND LESSONS TO LEARN

Whether you're seeking to master the ever-elusive perfect launch or looking to up your marketing game, there may be no better place to spend your educational dollars than the 20Books Vegas annual conference—and this year's event made it clear.

Do you need help with your newsletter? The presentations on newsletter list hygiene and keeping people signed up to your newsletter were just a couple of sessions that offered help in that field. Are you ready to dive into audio? "New Author Tips for Getting into Audio" was a worthwhile panel presentation, as was the session on Spotify & Findaway Voices. If you were looking to improve your series read-through, "Better Readthrough, Higher Royalties" was the presentation for you.

This conference not only brings a vast indie presence, but it also has drawn the attention of publishers as well. The Fantasy Pitch hosted by LMBPN this year was a popular pitch fest for four publishers looking to expand their author groups. The small room ended up packed wall to wall with people eager to see the process.

The newest trends in writing, beats, tropes, and reader expectation are available in concentrated form at the 20Books Vegas show. Having access to personnel from Kobo, Google Play, Amazon Vella, and many more is such a rare opportunity these days, and most of us struggle with platforms and algorithms where no human being is available. Not so at the conference, where authors could find real, honest-to-goodness people who helped work out issues and advised them how to move forward, both at Vendor Day on Monday and during platform-specific sessions.

The entire effort of the show and theme is also leveling up from year to year. Most who attend the annual 20Books conference make a list of things that they would like to accomplish the following year before they return. In truth, we are very lucky if we find ourselves halfway through the list before it's time to attend again in November. From the newly added young author presence to the uplifting and motivational opening speech by conference organizer Craig Martelle, the high-powered six-figure author panel, and the keynote address from 20BooksTo50K® co-founder Micheal Anderle, this year's conference contained all the tools an author might need to grow their business, plus many more that they didn't realize were crucial to authoring success.

But, as even the show leaders will attest, the true golden nuggets are always found in the hallways, standing in line for the cake machine, or at a little table outside of the grand event hall. Impromptu gatherings like this year's early morning sprints, genre dinners, and trips to the Thunder from Down Under show for the Romance authors are just a small fraction of the activities that lend themselves to finding your new best friend and that piece of missing information that changes everything.

Every effort was made to meet the needs of the aspiring author and provide information to help them move forward. The leaders set the tone, but the nearly two thousand members who attended were the force that kept the spirit of generosity and volunteerism alive throughout this year's conference.

Terry Wells-Brown

THE MAGIC OF CONFERENCE CONNECTIONS

I've never been to afternoon tea before, and you probably wouldn't think of Las Vegas as the place to try it for the first time. But I tell you, there was magic in that teapot.

On the Sunday before the 20Books Vegas 2022 conference started, my writing sisters and I met at the most delightful café for tea and tiny sandwiches. One member of our group, a teacher, asked what we wanted to get out of the conference. As we went around the table and answered, it struck me how each of us wanted to connect with different people. My goal was to meet other authors in my niche genre. One wanted to talk to those in the know about creating audiobooks. Another was keen to learn all they could about marketing and had a long list of questions to ask the presenters.

As if the teapot heard those wishes and determined to make

them come true, the conference was full of those magic connections. I overheard people making an audiobook deal in the Grand Salon between sessions. Authors solved website snafus over lunch. While munching on tacos and fajitas, I was invited to join a small group of authors in a narrow niche in my genre full of voracious readers. One author found some collaborating opportunities, which have the potential to really change the arc of his authoring business.

A struggling Thriller author received encouragement from renowned Thriller author Marc Cameron. 20BooksTo50K® co-founder Craig Martelle was joined at the conference by his dad, who livened up the event as authors competed for the best selfie in the conference's Facebook group. Romance and Women's Fiction author Elana Johnson signed autographs for her fans. And on Thursday, the Tiara Club drew over fifty authors together to celebrate their sparkly headwear.

Everywhere I looked, I saw authors making new friends, taking risks, and talking to their idols. From breakfast at Mon Ami Gabi to zip-lining and karaoke to dinner at Ping Pang Pong, authors packed their days full of opportunities to make those connections. And as if the magic from the teapot was still guiding us, the people we met at 20Books Vegas this year reminded each of us of the most important reward author conferences have to offer.

Robyn Sarty

SOMETHING TO RAVE ABOUT

Psst! Did you go to that massive RAVE in November?

The Readers & Authors Vegas Event (RAVE) takes place on the Friday following the end of the 20Books Vegas conference. This second year of the event was an even bigger hit than it was in 2021, with a greater number of attending authors and a larger influx of readers.

THE ATTENDEES

More than three hundred eager, smiling authors and several vendors attended this event with their books, and the day was, as expected, filled with buzz, excitement, and high energy. The attending authors brought their A game, with tables neatly decorated with books, treats, goodies, and giveaways. Many authors also dressed the part. Event-goers encountered dragons and fairy-tale princesses. A few narrators could be spotted in the wild as well. A couple of authors in the Horror section also had bodysuits cleverly printed with book covers.

Over one hundred fifty tables were jam-packed with books, and many were shared between two authors. These genre-based pairings allowed new and emerging authors to rub elbows—and create new friendships—with established authors in their genres.

THE VARIETY

RAVE saw nearly every genre represented at its booths, with authors from Sci-Fi, Fantasy, Horror, Thrillers, and nonfiction greeting readers. The Romance aisles especially overflowed with authors specializing in a vast array of subgenres, offering a little something for every book lover brave enough to dare such walks of true temptation.

THE ATMOSPHERE

Readers and authors alike shined with joy as they indulged in their mutual love of literature. Strained arms cradled book hauls, and those who brought book bags filled them to the brink. Many of us who flew home did so with luggage bursting at the seams or on luggage belts because of all the delicious titles so expertly displayed to win our hearts and minds.

Overall, RAVE was the perfect cherry on top of the sundae that is 20Books Vegas and a delightful way to wrap up the conference. Many of us are already looking forward to next year's RAVE with book-shaped stars glittering in our eyes. ∎

Audrey Hughey

Mark Your Calendar for These

More than a month has passed since 20Books Vegas 2022 came to an end. The nearly two thousand authors who attended have returned home and come down from the high of participating in the biggest indie author conference in the world. But for those same attendees, the lessons and new friends that came from the weeklong event will certainly last well into the new year.

It's only January, but plenty of authors worldwide are already looking to the new year for how they can reproduce that high that comes from being surrounded by their peers and the best minds in the industry. To help, we're rounding up some of the can't-miss events already scheduled for 2023. Mark your calendars, and don't forget to keep an eye out in the coming months for news on the next Author Tech Summit, hosted by *Indie Author Magazine*, and how you can sign up.

SUPERSTARS WRITING SEMINARS:

When: February 8–11, 2023
Where: Colorado Springs, Colorado
Cost: $899.99
Find out more at https://superstarswriting.com.

INDIE INSPIRATION:

When: March 24 and 25, 2023
Where: Virtual
Cost: $299 to $399
Find out more at https://indie-inspiration.teachable.com.

20BOOKS SPAIN:

When: April 13 and 14, 2023
Where: Seville, Spain
Registration is open now at http://20booksspain.com.
Follow the 20BooksTo50K® Facebook page for more information.

20BOOKS HOLLAND:

When: April 15 and 16, 2023
Where: Amsterdam, Netherlands
Cost: €185 to €225
Registration is open now. Find out more at http://20booksholland.com/selfpublishing-worldwide.

LONDON BOOK FAIR:

When: April 18–20, 2023
Where: London, UK
Emphasis on traditional publishing resources and organizations
Find out more at https://londonbookfair.co.uk/en-gb.html.

2023 Author Events

INKERS CON:

When: June 9–11, 2023
Where: Dallas, Texas
Cost: $649
Find out more at https://inkerscon.com.

INDIE UNCONFERENCE - EUROPE

When: June 14, 2023 at 7:30 p.m.
Where: Matera, Italy
Cost: €185-€225
Find out more at https://www.eventbrite.com/e/
indie-unconference-europe-tickets-463517953677.

SELF PUBLISHING SHOW LIVE:

When: June 20 and 21, 2023
Where: London, UK
Cost: £175 to £199
Find out more at https://selfpublishingformula.com/
spslive.

WHEN WORDS COLLIDE:

When: August 4–6, 2023
Where: Calgary, Alberta, Canada
Cost: $45 CAD
Find out more at https://whenwordscollide.org.

NOVELISTS, INC. (NINC) CONFERENCE:

When: September 20–24, 2023
Where: St. Pete Beach, Florida
Open to Novelists, Inc. members only
Find out more at https://ninc.com/conferences/
future-conferences.

FRANKFURT BOOK FAIR:

When: October 18–22, 2023 (The first three
days are trade days, with the final two days
open to public.)
Where: Frankfurt, Germany
Emphasis on traditional publishing resources
and organizations
Registration will open this month. Find out more at
https://www.buchmesse.de/en.

20BOOKS VEGAS:

When: November 6–10, 2023
Where: Las Vegas, Nevada
Cost: $349.99 to $499.99
Registration will open in January 2023. Follow the
20BooksTo50K® Facebook page for more information.

Which conferences and events are you planning on attending in 2023? Are there any we missed? Let us know at Events@indieauthormagazine.com! ■

Robyn Sarty

Five Plotting Methods You Can Use in Your Daily Life

It's a brand new year and, if you haven't done it already, it's a great time to make a plan for your author business. If you're a plotter, you probably already know plenty of planning methods like the back of your heart for outlining your novel, from Save the Cat to the Snowflake Method. But have you ever thought of using one or more of those same outlining methods for plotting out your business? Pantsers, take note—even if your drafts steer their own courses, your author career might benefit from some extra direction from time to time. And when your book business needs an outline, what better method to use than the ones that drive our stories?

Below, we're sharing possible ways you could do that, whether you're a Type A organizer or prefer to let your characters drive the ship. Try one of our examples on how to map out your 2023, or use them as a source of inspiration before creating a system of your own. It just might be the most important story you write this year.

1) THE SNOWFLAKE METHOD

With this method, start by summing up your novel with just one sentence. Expand that sentence to a one-paragraph summary, then a one-page summary, including goals and motivations for each character. Over the next stages, continue expanding your character descriptions further and deeper until you can produce a four-page overview of your novel.

You're now at the point where you know your characters well and have a synopsis that can be easily expanded into scenes.

There's a little more to the Snowflake Method than that—if you're not familiar with it, you can read more from its creator, Randy Ingermanson, on his website, https://www.advancedfictionwriting.com. But now, looking at that plan for a novel, it's not too difficult to see how you could use the same process to plan your goals for this year.

Start off small with just one sentence to describe what you want out of your year and where you want to be by the end of December. Many people choose just one word, such as "abundance," "inspiration," or "creativity" to focus on for their year, and you can do that here too.

You could use the single-paragraph summary to get excited about your goals and what you want to achieve, then write your own "character description" and look deeply at what motivates you, what stops you from moving forward and how you can overcome that, and where, and who, you really want to be.

Your four-page expanded summary could be your chance to imagine what your year will look like if you achieve everything you want in your life and in your author business, along with the beginnings of the steps you'll take to achieve that.

Finally, where you'd normally break your four-page summary down into scenes, instead, take your goals and break them down into manageable, achievable steps. Once you're at that stage, it's easier to plot those steps in your planner to make a working plan that can propel you to life and author success.

2) CHARACTER SHEETS

Most of us have probably spent time answering questions about our characters before we started writing our books, and character sheets with pre-written questions can be a handy way to do that. However, have you considered using a character sheet to help you with your author branding?

Here's the thing with branding: You might think that you don't have a brand, but you do. Your audience already has an opinion about who you are and what you're like from what you write, how you write it, and how you come across on social media. If you don't decide what you want your brand to be, your audience will make up their minds for you.

When building a brand, it's important to look at your business's personality, to understand what language the business would use if it were a person and to learn how it would speak, how it would react to the world, and how it would want to be seen—the same set of details you seek to understand when developing a new protagonist.

To start, think about what words you might use to describe your author business, just as you might do with your characters. Is your business cool, edgy, trendy, and elegant, or is it warm, humorous, and friendly, with a messy bun?

Although you can't control what other people think, you can decide what you want your author brand to be and then consistently put that image out there, leaving you far more in control of how your author brand is seen. Check out Reedsy's blog post on character development as an example, and download the site's character sheet or use a similar template to give it a try: https://blog.reedsy.com/character-profile.

The same character sheets that help you create realistic characters that leap off the page can help you nail your author brand too.

3) SAVE THE CAT

Screenwriter Blake Snyder originally created his Save the Cat story-telling method for himself and fellow screenwriters. Snyder felt he needed help during the second act of the traditional three-act structure, where there seemed to be a lot of space to fill between the first and third acts. To fix the issue, he expanded the three-act structure to <u>fifteen beats</u> in order to give him more points from which to ground his story, during what might otherwise be the saggy middle. Why is it called Save the Cat? Because Snyder wanted to ensure that the viewer or reader related to the main character and liked them. He wanted them to "save the cat" to give them a moment right at the beginning to endear themselves to the audience or reader.

Over time, Snyder's method has become one of the more popular ways to plot a novel, but there's no reason you can't use the same beats to plan out your year too.

Although it doesn't always feel like it, there's an awful lot of time to fill between January 1 and December 31 of a new year. Why not use your own beats as goals or steps to aim for, broken down over the year so that your time is more effectively spent and you don't have too many things happening at once?

For the coming year, try writing each of your goals in a couple of sentences. Then divide them into a series of fifteen—or any number you choose—steps before plotting how and when you'll get there in your calendar.

4) THE DAN HARMON STORY CIRCLE

Dan Harmon's Story Circle starts with a character in their comfort zone at the beginning of a story. Over eight steps, the character goes on a journey, physical or emotional, and ultimately returns to the beginning having changed.

The steps are as follows:

1. Character is in their comfort zone.
2. Character wants something and decides to take action.
3. Character finds themself in an unfamiliar situation.
4. Character adapts to the new situation.
5. Character gets what they want.
6. Character pays a heavy price for what they wanted.
7. Character returns to where they started, but …
8. … character has changed.

That might be a great plan for story structure, but we think it also sums up what happens when stretching ourselves and reaching for big goals. Although you don't necessarily pay a big price for reaching for your goals—hopefully, you won't, anyway—it's likely that you will learn and change along the way.

If you've got big goals for this year, think about this structure, and use it to plan how you'll get to where you want to be by the end of the year. You can follow the same eight steps you did for your novel:

1. Know your comfort zone. What do you enjoy about your current situation?
2. What do you want? Choose your goals and how you want to change.
3. Take action. Plan out what steps you need to take and write what you need to reach your goals, then start following your plan.
4. Adapt. You'll likely end up in unfamiliar territory, but that was the point.
5. Do the work. Now that you're here, how can you learn and grow to get what you want? Are there courses you need to take or people you need to connect with? Find out what you need to do to bring you closer to your goals.
6. Pay the price? Hopefully, you can skip this step or at least limit your "price" to the cost of whichever courses or materials you bought previously.
7. Celebrate. You did it! Acknowledge that and take time to let it sink in. Reward yourself for getting to this point.
8. Return to Step 1. Go back to the beginning and think about what you want next. Choose your next goal with all the new knowledge you've picked up in reaching your first goal.

If you're not great at working on multiple goals at once, a plan like this where you focus on just one goal and then choose another may work better for you.

5) THE FICHTEAN CURVE

Looking at the Fichtean Curve for the first time, you might wonder why on earth we'd choose it as a possible strategy for achieving your goals. Authors generally reserve this method of outlining for Mysteries and breathless Thrillers that build to a huge climax. The diagram's curve starts with rising action for the first two-thirds of the story, then builds to the big climax, which is followed by falling action that continues until the end of the book. The idea is to get the story going immediately with action taking place from the beginning.

When plotted out, the Fichtean Curve divides a story into Crisis 1, Crisis 2, Crisis 3, Crisis 4, Crisis 5, Climax, and Falling Action. Of course, we're not wishing crisis after crisis on you or your author careers, but consider shaping your business plan into a series of several steps that continually propel you toward a big achievement—your author career's climax.

This planning method works especially well for the biggest and most daunting goals that we have. Choose your massive goal and then break down the steps you need in place to get to it. After that, just keep pushing the boulder up the hill and persevering until you do.

There's one final outlining method that can be of great use when making plans to achieve any goal: reverse outlining. With this method, authors begin by writing how their novel ends. Then, once they know the ending, they're able to walk the story backward step by step until they reach the beginning. The same method is a great way to find the steps you'll need to take to reach your goals. You know where you're going and what you want to achieve, so break it down and work it out backward from your end goal to your starting point. Then, find out how long you'll need to reach each step, and mark the corresponding dates in your planner.

Whatever method you use for planning out your year, we hope we've given you some food for thought and maybe some new methods for taking your author business to the next level. ∎

Gill Fernley

A Tale of Three Presses

IS YOUR PUBLISHING MISSION BUILT TO LAST?

Children's author Marti Dumas (https://martidumasbooks.com) is an indie publisher who started her career with a clear mission: to provide specific books for specific readers. In some ways, her mission hasn't changed at all. When her six-year-old ran out of books and started taking Jonathan Swift off the family bookcase, Dumas decided to write an age-appropriate book as a Christmas-turned-Kwanzaa present. Her daughter loved *Jala and the Wolves* and shared it with the neighborhood. Of course, when the younger child turned six, he also wanted his own personal book.

There was only one problem.

As an educator, Dumas knew that her youngest needed a different kind of book. "He needed something that was … specifically for kids like him. … Preferably brown, but not necessarily," she says. The book needed to match his love for science, his humor, and his search for adventure. But the answer posed a different sort of challenge for Dumas.

"[I realized] 'Oh, but I can't actually write this because the actual correct book for him would need to be … an illustrated chapter book,'" Dumas says. If the book needed artwork, she'd need collaborators to bring it to life.

Thankfully, she wasn't the only person who recognized a need for the book. "Things happened," Dumas says, in her understated way, "people put money in, and we ended up forming a small mission-driven press, which is Plum Street Press that publishes books that feature children of color, where race is not the conflict in the story." The time to start a publishing house came when its scope grew big enough to include new partners. A short while later, the New Orleans-based boutique children's book press was born.

Dumas' path into the book world might seem unorthodox to some, but her ever-growing list of roles and titles today speaks to her success. From becoming a co-owner of a publishing house in order to release her debut book to finding a home for her later series with traditional publishers, her story also offers a lesson to other authors who seek to follow in her footsteps: namely, that there aren't always footsteps to follow.

VISION + NETWORK + SKILLS

Most authors don't begin their indie author careers with the business side, but Dumas had a clear vision for her work, a healthy network of friends, and an impressive set of skills. "I am a teacher and also a consultant and an organizer," she says. "So … the idea of making a company that doesn't have a specific mission seems foolish to me." She chose her direction and stuck with it, and in 2017, she gave a podcast interview about forming Plum Street Press (https://plumstreetpressbooks.com) to publish *Jala and the Wolves* and the *Jaden Toussaint, the Greatest* series.

Her deep understanding of her target audience might be one key to her ongoing motivation. "I was a classroom teacher for thirteen years, and ten of those are in elementary school," she says. "That is my sweet spot for fiction because [fourth and fifth grade is] … perfectly middle grade."

Finding books for the kids in her classroom fine-tuned her ability to choose strong story ideas, both in her own writing and the books she publishes through her press. "That's almost always where my stories start … [with] a kid that I know who needed a story."

Dumas' experience in the book world doesn't stop with her own author career or even with Plum Street Press. As an audiobook narrator who speaks English and French and handles a variety of dialects and accents, Dumas has other skills and connections to

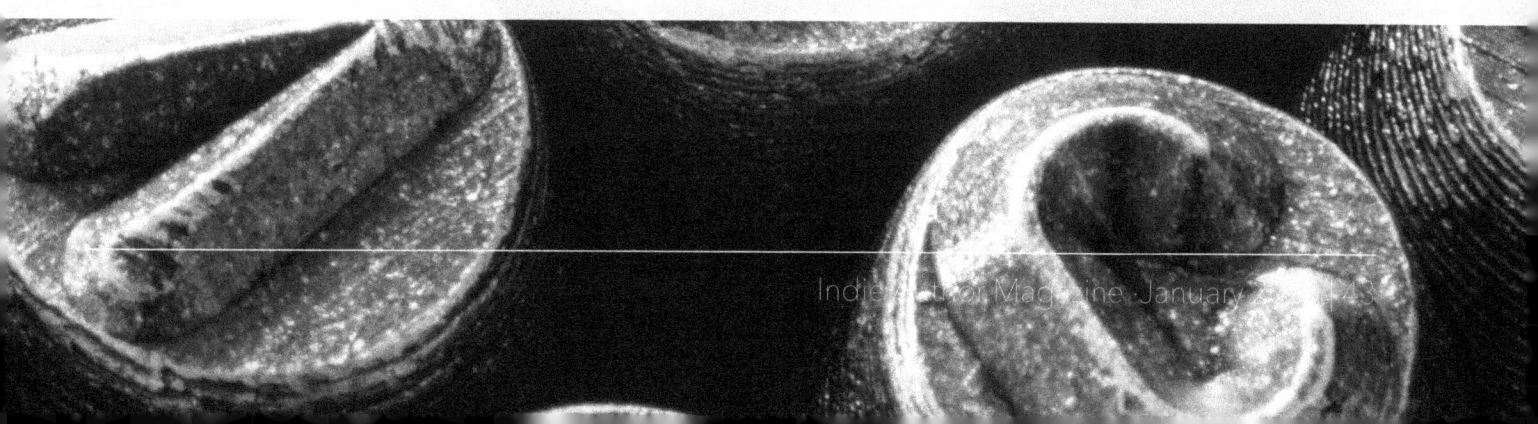

the publishing universe. Although not looking for an agent, she met one at a friend's party who asked her to submit—then asked again a few months later when Dumas, thinking the offer was polite conversation, hadn't followed through. After all, why would a successful indie author and co-owner of a publishing house choose to go back into the query trenches?

She knew she would have to have just the right project, because some manuscripts need more creative control than others. Dumas says, "My *Seeds of Magic* series I would never have submitted because I am completely uninterested in anyone else's opinion on that story." But when she started working on a different series, *Wildseed Witch,* she realized she would be willing to share creative control over the new story. "[This project] could use other eyes … maybe shaping the direction that the story might go," she says. "And I just wanted to see what that [traditional publishing] process was like."

Although willing to invite other perspectives into her creative process, Dumas is working from a position of strength because of her experience as an indie author. "[To publish traditionally] you need a project that you're like, 'I'm totally willing to collaborate but also I can do it on my own' because you don't know what kind of editor you are going to get."

HOW MUCH CONTROL DO YOU NEED?

In a surprising plot twist, publishing traditionally turns out to be another way Plum Street Press achieves its mission. "It's very important to me and the other people who invested in the Plum Street Press for us to make the books as easily available to all kids as possible," Dumas says. "That means being in as many venues as possible, which means taking down as many invisible walls as we can between us and the venues." A traditionally published book is eligible for awards, editorial reviews, and other forms of recognition that may encourage libraries, schools, and parents to purchase it for their collections. But that recognition may be impossible for an indie author or a boutique publisher like Plum Street Press.

Dumas is a co-owner of her publishing company, but as an author/publisher with successful books, it makes sense to pursue a broader audience with a mainstream publisher. As Dumas says, "knowing why you're doing the thing … is really important because you're going to have missteps. You're going to have things that don't go quite the direction that you thought or you're going to try a foray with big pub, and maybe you don't love it. I'm so far okay, but at any moment I could … be like … 'I don't want to deal with this ever again.' But I know that I'm not going to quit writing books for kids and publishing them because I have a reason to be doing it."

With Dumas' current publishing deals with both Amulet and Scholastic, the potential for taking down invisible walls is high. Last year, Amulet—the publisher of the popular middle grade series *Diary of a Wimpy Kid*—published the first book in Dumas' *Wildseed Witch* series, with book two set to release in May 2023. Meanwhile, Dumas' nonfiction title, *Women in the Old West*, is backed by the hundred-year-old publisher Scholastic, famous for school fundraisers in the form of in-school book fairs in the United States. The ethos of Scholastic in particular aligns with the Plum Street Press mission. <u>As reported by *Publishing Perspectives*</u>, the President and CEO of Scholastic, Peter Warwick, spoke at last month's Frankfurt Book Fair about the importance of marketing diverse books: "As publishers, we must avoid saying 'We need to publish diverse books' and then put them into a separate section and market them less. We need to say, 'This is part of our mainstream, and make sure that we market them effectively.'"

As a successful indie author and publisher, Dumas has a completely different relationship with her "big pub" houses than the typical debut author. "It makes a way better time for me to try it and see what it's all about. Because I don't actually have a fear of being ostracized from publishing because I was never in," she says. "I'm doing my own thing, and I'm not going to stop because I have a very focused mission."

"I think that there is a lot to be learned from working with big publishers," Dumas continues, adding that "some … are reinforcements of lessons that I thought that I already had." For example, for authors doing a "foray into big publishing, you are going to need to know how to market your books, because even when they're marketing your books, you are the biggest asset to them, not your books."

LESSONS LEARNED

Looking back at the growth of Plum Street Press, Dumas would tell her past self to outsource tasks earlier. As an educator, she enjoyed learning new skills, and she still thinks it's valuable to be familiar with the tasks you are outsourcing, but not an expert, adding that "you should be like a ten of diamonds of all trades just so that you can supervise people that you hire."

She also advised that indie authors learn "the secret nods and whistles" of the publishing industry to keep your books from being immediately discarded by the audiences you're trying to reach. "For example," Dumas says, "Tuesday is pub day. When you release your book on a different day, you signal to all the librarians and schools that your book isn't a traditionally published book." The advice goes for authors who write for all genres and age groups—bookstores like Kobo pay attention to your publish date as well.

Most importantly, authors and publishers need to understand the expectations they're setting for their readers with every project they take on. Ironically, Dumas had to make the publishing case for her *Seeds of Magic* series for grades three through six to her own publishing house. The other co-owners of Plum Street Press expected her to write more books similar to her original *Jaden Toussaint* series. Dumas had to demonstrate that her new books were a "smart expansion of the brand" and fit the original mission of Plum Street Press. To a solo indie author, it might seem pointless to go through this kind of traditional publishing exercise, but it got everyone at the press on the same page and helped them support the books together. This cohesion is why literary agents and editors at conferences ask authors, "Why did you write this book?"

Branding isn't just beneficial for marketing either. Interestingly, as a result of its brand expansion into fantasy genre for slightly older kids, Plum Street Press attracted "more authors to us … who were ready" to publish, Dumas says, "because a lot of times people are excited [about publishing] and they're pre-ready." Today, in addition to publishing Dumas' books, Plum Street Press publishes middle grade adventures and nonfiction for ages four and up by other authors.

ONE MISSION; MANY PATHS

Dumas still isn't following a single path up the publishing mountain. She's diversifying to take advantage of all opportunities to achieve her publishing mission and serve her audience. Amulet releases Dumas' *Charmed Life*, book two in the *Wildseed Witch* series, on May 2, 2023. Later that month, *Book of Dragons*, the latest book in Dumas' *Seeds of Magic* series, comes out with Plum Street Press. So what's the target for this wide-thinking author and publisher? "Forty-nine," she whips out, with a big smile. "Forty-nine books for kids."

Both Marti Dumas and Darcy Pattison, another children's book author and publisher, have similar publishing stories: They both bring all their talents, skills, and connections to the publishing table. The message for indie authors is clear: You don't have to define yourself as an author by the way you publish—even if you have your own publishing house.

Do you want to do everything you can to reach your audience? Or do you want to do it all on your own? There's no single right answer, just as Marti Dumas' mind-bending example proves. ∎

Laurel Decher

Otter.ai

AN AUTHOR'S STARTING PLACE FOR SPEECH-TO-TEXT SOFTWARE

A plethora of AI programs and apps have appeared in the last few years, SPARKING varying opinions about <u>what they mean for creative industries</u>. However, some AI tools can be helpful and have already been integrated into daily use for years with little fanfare. Otter.ai, a popular transcription service that operates using AI, is one such example. Founded in 2016, Otter is a text-to-speech software that records audio and transcribes voice conversations in real time using AI technology.

Otter, like most transcription services, is not designed specifically with authors in mind; instead, the app was originally meant to serve as a transcription service for business meetings. The primary focus of the program, as shared on the company's website, is to "capture and share insights from your meetings." The paragraph below explains, "Otter records meetings, takes notes in real time, and generates an automated summary to share with everyone and to help you remember everything."

So this is clearly a note-taking app designed for the workplace to allow meeting participants to focus on collaborating and engaging with each other, without having to worry about taking notes. However, even though this is not a tool designed to help authors specifically, there are ways Otter could make your writing life easier and more efficient.

WHAT IS IT FOR?

You can use Otter to record and transcribe conversations on your mobile phone or web browser using the built-in microphone. If you wish, you can then share your conversations with others for them to view or edit.

Additionally, unlike some voice-to-text apps and software, users can connect Otter to Zoom, Microsoft Teams, or Google Meet to take and share notes automatically. This could be invaluable for authors who are working with a writing coach. There's no need to take copious notes, because Otter can take care of those for you.

In fact, this is how I first got to know Otter. I worked with a coach who used Otter to audio record the meeting and provide a transcription—a different method than the one I'd used to provide recordings for my own clients, which involved uploading the recordings to YouTube as unlisted videos. With Otter, meeting recordings can be made available much faster and require no public upload.

Otter's transcription feature also makes it easy for clients to skim the text and then head to a specific point in the audio if they want to listen again to what was said. With a YouTube video, you have to watch through the full meeting, though that site does also offer AI-generated transcriptions and captions with a few additional steps.

Nonfiction authors who do a lot of interviews for their books may also find Otter useful, as would any author who does interviews for general research. Not only can Otter take notes for you, but you can then copy and paste relevant parts of the transcription straight into your manuscript.

But you don't need to be working with other people to find Otter useful; it can also be used as dictation software. With <u>Dragon Professional software</u> costing five hundred dollars, not including additional equipment like a quality microphone, Otter offers a low-cost alternative to some of the more well-known apps for those who like to record voice notes or dictate their books.

Pro Tip: For iOS 13, you can create a Siri Shortcut to start recording in Otter as follows:

1. Install and open the iOS Shortcuts app.
2. Tap on "Create Shortcut."
3. Tap on the three-dot icon to name the shortcut.
4. Tap on "Add Action."
5. Search for "Otter."
6. Tap on "Start recording."
7. Tap on "Done."

WHAT DOES IT COST?

Otter has a free basic plan, so you can give the program a try at no cost and without providing credit card details. If you don't require many transcription minutes per month, the Basic plan may suit your needs just fine. The Pro plan is also available for individuals who need more minutes and offers users a few extra features.

The Basic plan includes three hundred monthly transcription minutes with a limit of thirty minutes per conversation, whereas the Pro plan offers twelve hundred monthly transcription minutes with a ninety-minute cap per conversation.

Basic
For individuals just getting started

Free

[Get Started]

- Record and transcribe your meetings in real time
- Otter Assistant joins Zoom, Microsoft Teams, and Google Meet to automatically take and share notes, even if you can't join the meeting
- Takeaways and Automated Summary
- 300 monthly transcription minutes; 30 minutes per conversation

Pro
For individuals who need more minutes and features

$8.33 USD per month

Billed Annually [Save 51%]

[Buy Now]

Everything in Basic +

- Import and transcribe pre-recorded audio or video files
- Otter Assistant joins meetings when you are double-booked
- Advanced search, export, and playback
- 1200 monthly transcription minutes; 90 minutes per conversation

Business
For small teams and organizations that need to share & collaborate

$20 USD per user/month

Billed Annually [Save 33%]

[Buy Now]

Everything in Pro +

- Team features: shared custom vocabulary and speakers, assign action items to teammates
- Otter Assistant joins meetings when you are triple-booked
- Admin features: usage analytics, centralized billing, prioritized support
- 6000 monthly transcription minutes; 4 hours per conversation

The Business plan is designed for teams and will likely be unnecessary for most authors. It could be useful for nonfiction authors who do a lot of interviews; however, heavy users may find another, more advanced service will better suit their needs.

The Pro plan is $16.99 per month, or $99.99 if you choose to pay annually, which offers a 51 percent savings. The Business plan is thirty dollars per month, per user.

Additional features in the Pro plan that may be useful to authors include:

- Custom Vocabulary: The free plan allows users to add up to five terms, such as for names, jargon, or acronyms; the Pro plan allows for one hundred names plus one hundred other terms.
- Playback Speeds: The free plan only offers standard playback, while users can choose from eight different speeds in the Pro plan, slowing down a recording by as much as half speed or speeding it up to as much as three times the original playback speed. Pro plan users also have the option to skip past silence in the recording automatically.

Even with these additional features, the minutes allowance is likely to be the biggest deciding factor when choosing whether to upgrade to the Pro plan.

HOW ACCURATE IS IT?

Otter transcriptions are certainly not without errors. In fact, compared to Rev.com, another speech-to-text transcription service, it is far less accurate. If I were using the service to take notes on meetings I were unable to attend, I'm not confident that the transcription could accurately fill me in. However, when reviewing my own recordings where I know what was said, it is easy to edit the transcription file. In addition, you can easily jump to any point in the audio to have a listen if you need to clarify anything that looks strange.

No AI transcription software offers one hundred percent accuracy, and accuracy is also affected by things like the quality of your recording equipment and how clear the

---

SUMMARY KEYWORDS

work, programme, people, emails, bit, feel, book, va, sales, content, thinking, client, starting, coaching, questions, launch, authors, point, pitch, selling

SPEAKERS

Speaker 2, Speaker 1

Speaker 1 0:12

I'm not on Video Hello, I've just I've just started up otter and realised that I hadn't stopped it from the last client and I've now got me singing Bon Jovi on the end

0:27

that client call

Speaker 1 0:31

so hopefully you won't listen to that it's got 15 minutes of me singing Bon Jovi and

0:39

doo doo doo and chuck it could

Speaker 1 0:48

have done worse one time. At the end of the sales call. I said I love you to somebody. I felt that she had a vibe like my sister like I was on the phone to my sister. I can imply their love you know what I just said?

Speaker 2 1:06

Well, you know, it's you came about your time I really

1:09

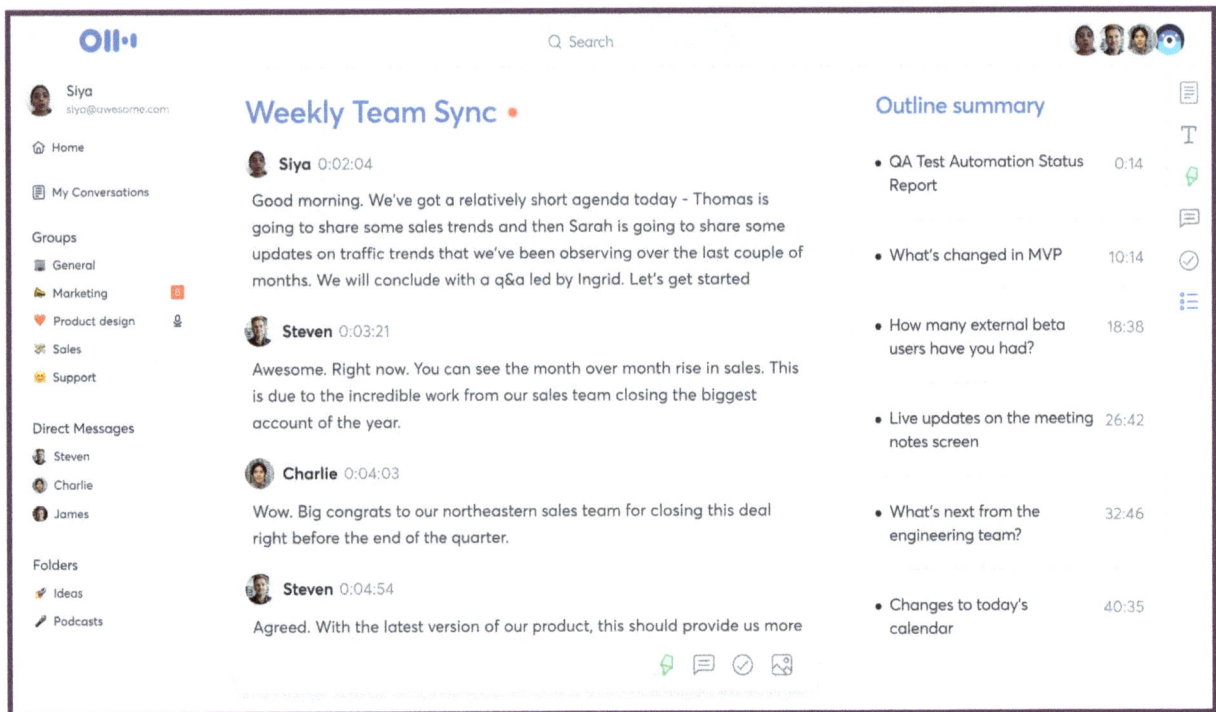

speakers are. But if you're looking for something that can transcribe your voice notes quickly and provide a rough-and-ready document for you to work with, Otter is likely to be good enough for your needs.

Pro Tip: With the Otter mobile app, you can record conversations and receive notifications on all your devices. Plus, everything is synced, so what you do on one device is reflected everywhere.

Two other important things to note: Otter only supports transcription in English, and it only offers email support. If getting on the phone with someone or live chat is important to you if you have technical issues, Otter will not be a good fit.

WHAT ARE THE ALTERNATIVES?

Depending on how you want to use Otter, there are alternatives to consider. For example, if you only want to use it for voice notes, the Gboard app for iOS or Android is a simple, free option.

To use Gboard on your phone, simply follow the steps below:

1. Install Gboard.
2. Open any app where you can type, such as Gmail or Keep.
3. Tap an area where you can enter text.
4. Touch and hold the microphone icon.
5. When you see "Speak now," say what you want to be written.

You can also use the free Apple Dictation app for Apple devices or the free Windows 10 Speech Recognition app for Windows users. If you like using Google Docs, you can also try the program's voice typing feature, found as an add-on in the Extensions menu of the toolbar.

If you are more interested in Otter's ability to transcribe Zoom or MS Teams meetings in real time, then you may also want to check out Airgram, which supports multilingual transcription, or Fireflies.ai, which will support transcription in other languages soon, according to its website.

Finally, if you need much greater accuracy in your transcriptions, you may prefer a service like Rev.com, which offers human transcription for $1.50 per minute of audio. Or transcribe the audio on your own from a recorded audio file. Although it may take more time, in terms of accuracy, accessibility, and cost, AI still has yet to match the simplest transcription tool of all: your keyboard and your own ears. ■

Belinda Griffin

Download ^   Resources ⌄

Otter for iOS >
Download the app for all iOS devices

Otter for Android >
Download the app for all Android devices

Chrome extension >
Download to use Otter in your browser

Tech Tools

Courtesy of IndieAuthorTools.com
Got a tool you love and want to share with us?
Submit a tool at IndieAuthorTools.com

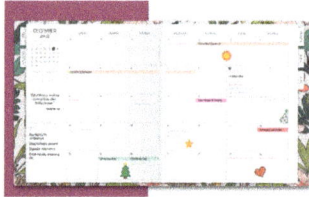

Artful Agenda

Combine the fun and personalization of a paper planner with the convenience of a digital calendar. Choose your cover design and handwriting, color code events, and personalize with stickers. Mobile & tablet apps now in Apple and Google Play stores. Syncs with Google, Apple, and Outlook.
https://artfulagenda.com/

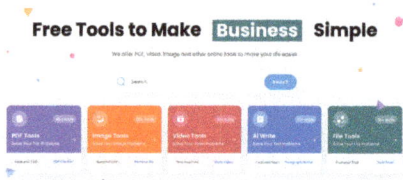

TinyWow

TinyWow is a website that offers a variety of free online tools to help users with a range of tasks and problems. Some of the key features of TinyWow include: PDF tools, video tools, image tools, and meme generator.
https://tinywow.com

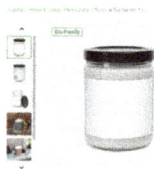

Printify

Printify simplifies and automates the process of sourcing and creating print on demand products at the best prices on the market. It integrates with the major direct-sales platforms, including Etsy, Shopify, WooCommerce, and Wix (among others) and offers unique items that other dropshipping companies don't.
https://printify.com

Magic Eraser

An online alternative to one of Photoshop's most popular features, Magic Eraser lets users upload an image and erase unwanted objects in seconds. Were your vacation photos photobombed? No problem – edit out the unwanted person in seconds. If only it worked in real life!
https://magicstudio.com/magiceraser

Repurpose.io

Repurpose.io is a useful tool for individuals and organizations looking to efficiently repurpose and publish content across multiple social media channels. Its wide range of input and output channels, along with the ability to easily create and manage workflows, makes it a valuable asset for anyone looking to streamline their content creation and distribution processes.

Habits of Seven-Figure Authors

What author doesn't dream of becoming a millionaire? Every writer wishes to have a tremendous income straight from their books, along with thousands of adoring readers. The mountain it takes to achieve such a pinnacle, however, can seem long and daunting, especially to authors who struggle to sell single copies of their title. These elusive writers who have such exceptional careers seem so high above the average traditionally published author, who, according to the <u>Authors Guild's 2018 Author Income Survey</u>, is likely to make twelve thousand dollars a year or less. So are there secret habits to success that these millionaire authors have discovered?

Rachel Hanna is willing to share her story. She is a successful seven-figure author of Women's Fiction. She writes Southern Romance books that center on stories about family and friendships, with characters who range in age from teenagers to middle-aged adults to characters in their eighties. "Older characters have interesting things going on in their lives, too, so I try to highlight them," she says. "It's not true, at least not for me, that you have to center your story around a young twenty-something." To date, her backlist includes almost forty books.

Hanna has a degree in journalism and worked in that field before she began working from home in many different areas. She was never a big reader but decided to write her first book in 2012 during the Kindle boom.

"I started publishing that same year and started making money," she says. "Then I had a personal crisis, believing that I wasn't a professional author, so I started trying to change everything in my business. I lost that momentum."

She turned to running an eBay business, which she describes as exhausting and frustrating. The job required her to work long hours every day of the week, which wasn't how she wanted to live her life.

"We were struggling. I hit the point where I was done, and I either had to give up or believe in myself and what I wanted to do. So in 2019, I decided to let everything go and focus on becoming a full-time author," Hanna says.

She told her husband to move everything eBay related out of her office, so she could use it for writing, and she completely abandoned all other projects in order to pursue a career in Women's Fiction. The change wasn't easy. Her backlist wasn't performing well, and there was no replacement income if her titles failed to sell.

"I didn't want to give myself a fallback, thinking that if it didn't work, I'd go back to something else," Hanna describes, "because if you're doing that, you're giving your brain a chance that it won't pan out, so I didn't give it any chance."

She thought about what a full-time author would do every day. She decorated her office like the setting of her novels, printed out a vision board of what she wanted to achieve, and posted notes on income goals everywhere she could see them.

"I tried to surround myself with successful people, who had the things I wanted," Hanna says. "I read and listened to only uplifting things—happy music, funny movies. I meditated until it put me into a whole different mindset, and that's what was different this time than all the other times I'd tried to make my author business work before. I looked at other authors doing big things and believed that I could be her."

One exercise, which she said was very helpful, was imagining herself having a conversation with another person about her success while replying to the conversation out loud. This helped to cement the concept in her head that her dreams could become a reality.

Hanna said she gave herself no option but to be successful, conquering a negative mindset she'd lived with for years. She wrote at restaurants, eating nachos while pantsing her stories and creating long series with multiple books.

"I started saying 'when this happens' instead of 'if this happens.' If you write a really good book one, your readers won't want to leave the world. Now, I'm on book ten, and the series is still going strong," Hanna says.

Her first major goal was to have a six-figure month in income. After she'd seen an author friend achieve this pinnacle, Hanna set herself on the same path.

"In September of 2019, I was only making around two thousand dollars a month from my books, and that's when I decided to go full time. By Christmas, we were about to lose our house, but I kept pursuing my dream," Hanna says. "In March the following year, I had been making thirty thousand dollars a month and didn't think I could go higher than that. That's when I closed all my other businesses to let myself know I was serious. By September of that year, I was making one hundred grand a month, and I've made a hundred grand a month ever since."

According to Hanna, her incredible income is because of her attention to mindset.

"You can have all the business know-how, but if you don't have a positive mindset, it's not going to work, or even if you attain that success, you won't be able to maintain it, because you'll get impostor syndrome," Hanna says. "I decided that being a seven-figure author is who I am, and once I did that, the impostor syndrome went away. I didn't leave any room for this not working out."

Her habits, in her own words, are scatterbrained yet make for an ingenious recipe for success. Every day is different for her, and she spends her time doing what she feels inspired to do rather than what she feels she must do.

"I am a very fly-by-the-seat-of-my-pants person. The truth is I can go days without writing, then I'll get inspired and write a few thousand words. When I try to be on a schedule, it stifles my creativity," Hanna says.

She encourages other authors to work with who they are and what their gifts are instead of attempting to force themselves to adapt habits that don't work for them. "What messed me up for years was trying to be like other people," Hanna says. "Every day is different as to what I'm doing. Some days, I'll work on ads. Other days, I'll work on building a direct sales system on my website. It's very dependent on what I feel like doing that day. There's no set routine."

Hanna does have a remedy for the days when she is down because, to her, being in a negative place can have the worst effect on her business.

"Sometimes I need a day to rest my mind. I'll spend the day journaling or watching happy movies because if you're in an overwhelmed funk, you can't work well," Hanna says. "Taking that time really helped because it enabled me to be creative again."

Hanna said that the most important thing for authors to keep in mind while attempting to grow their career is to have patience and not try to force something into being before its time.

"The fact that people try to force things will slow them down. They get angry it's not happening in their timeline," Hanna says. "It took me eight to ten years of writing to get where I am now, and all that time, I was working on my mindset. You can't give up after a year of getting discouraged. You have to let go of when you think it should happen because you can't see the bigger picture."

Detachment from the outcome, according to Hanna, is the key.

"If I had not struggled so much, I wouldn't have written the book that took off. I would've kept being comfortable, and that's where I got stuck. Put it in front of your face every day what you want to be, and put no thought into when or how it'll happen because if you hold on to something so tightly, it won't grow," Hanna says.

When asked what she wants her fellow writers to know, Hanna says that the most successful author habit any writer can have, above all, is holding on to your dream.

"I turned into the person I wanted to be because there was nowhere else to go. Now we have everything we want," Hanna says. "I don't believe in unrealistic goals. Don't play small and let your thoughts keep you from being successful, because who are you helping? Be as abundant as possible in order to be able to give as much as possible, and believe in yourself."

Rachel Hanna's books can be found at https://rachelhannaauthor.com. ■

Megan Linski-Fox

Podcasts We Love

Sell More Books Show
Authors, are you struggling to get the word out about your books? Discover the latest book marketing and publishing news, tools and strategies. This is the Sell More Books Show with H. Claire Taylorl and Bryan Cohen. Every week you'll get helpful tips and ideas to make your book sales soar. Visit Sell-MoreBooksShow.com for detailed show notes and more info.
https://writelink.to/sellmorebooksshow

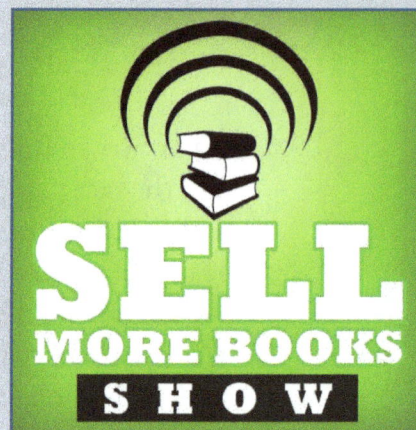

Mel Robbins Podcast
Kick off the New Year with a podcast designed to get you moving! Every episode of The Mel Robbins Podcast is filled with the motivation and tactics you need plus deeply personal stories, relatable topics and tactical, research-backed advice to help you create a better life.
https://www.melrobbins.com/podcast

20Booksto50K Live Events Channel
While not technically a podcast, most of these videos can be listened to without losing any of the great information. They're broken up into playlists including the Five-Minute Focus, and the presentations from nearly every 20Booksto50K conference.
https://www.youtube.com/@20Booksto50kRLiveEvents

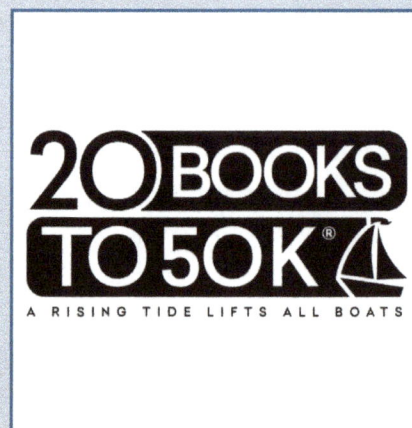

How Your Characters' Needs Can Make Them More Human

I opened the revisions file from my editor on my latest work in progress and was surprised by the number one item on her list. "The protagonist is launching a business!" she wrote. "Why isn't she working on her website, having business cards made, handing out flyers—anything?"

I was slightly insulted. Of course, my character was doing whatever she needed to get her business off to a successful start. But there had just been a murder. Wasn't that more important?

After I'd smoothed down my ruffled feathers, I realized my editor was right. I'd been so caught up in making my protagonist a sleuth that I'd neglected to make her human. I went back through the draft and made sure to show the character working on that website, ordering inventory, advertising, and becoming familiar with the neighborhood in which her shop was located.

The need for more mundane details doesn't just apply to business ventures. Your readers want to know where your characters sleep, what they eat, and how they take care of their pets. If you've ever read a Cozy Mystery, you'll know some readers care so much about what the characters eat, they insist on recipes being included at the back of the book.

If your character wandered through the desert all day and night with no food or water, he or she shouldn't show up at a battle scene the next morning fresh, alert, and ready to fight. And if your protagonist is an alien or superhero who doesn't need sleep, food, or water, you need to make that apparent ahead of time.

WHAT EXACTLY DOES YOUR CHARACTER NEED?

Maslow's Hierarchy of Needs is a theory in the field of psychology proposed in 1943 by Abraham Maslow that suggests people will prioritize their most basic needs ahead of more advanced goals (https://www.simplypsychology.org/maslow.html). The theory is most often depicted as a pyramid, with the bottom of the pyramid showing the basic needs—water, food, shelter, and sleep. Knowing how these needs, whether met or unmet, will affect your story facilitates your creation of a well-rounded character.

Look at the 2002 movie *Insomnia*. The detective in that movie suffers from sleep deprivation while investigating a murder in Alaska, and it drastically hampers his ability to solve the crime. Like with other physiological needs in Maslow's pyramid, a character who cannot sleep will see those effects ripple outward into every other aspect of their lives, leading to problems such as stress, memory issues, and slower healing. And it won't necessarily take much time for it to do so.

Food can be as much a necessity as sleep for your characters, so make sure you give them a chance to eat and drink regularly. Of course, that's if they have access to either—but if they don't, it's well worth checking out resources on the long-term effects of food deprivation and hunger, such as Natalie Silver's breakdown of the question "How Long Can You Live Without Food?" on Healthline.com. Whether your protagonist is on a diet or visiting a foreign planet and having trouble finding food compatible with his or her body, you need to understand how he or she will feel and think based on this lack of nourishment.

And if one of your characters is unhoused—temporarily or otherwise—consider taking a look at the February 2019 report, "Homelessness & Health: What's the Connection?" by the National Health Care for the Homeless Council (https://nhchc.org) to understand the effects a lack of shelter has on one's physical and mental health.

The second tier of the needs hierarchy reflects safety needs. In modern settings, perhaps most important is how your character makes a living. Is he living off his savings while he avenges his father's murder? Is she married to an abusive billionaire and secretly looking for ways to escape? Is your character a child whose resources come from parents or other family members? In books that take place in more fantastical worlds, it might be more important to look beyond financial security. How does your character survive if your protagonist is living in a post-apocalyptic world or on another planet? Show your reader how your characters protect themselves and others—and what happens when they can't.

In the center of the Maslow's Hierarchy of Needs pyramid, we have love and belonging. Character relationships are central to almost any story, but they're also essential for understanding how your character experiences the world. Perhaps something has happened at the beginning of your story to stigmatize your character. In that case, show the reader your character's aching need for acceptance. If your character is established in the community, then don't forget to give them acquaintances. Even a lone lighthouse keeper would see a delivery person or regular angler on occasion. Alternatively, you might have characters who put the needs of their loved ones ahead of their own, such as in Charles Dickens' *A Tale of Two Cities*. These choices, even if they aren't acknowledged outright, can be especially impactful. By incorporating such scenes, you can illustrate the strength of certain character relationships to readers and make small moments, such as treating an injury or sharing a last bite of food, even more meaningful in the larger story.

Esteem and self-actualization are at the peak of the needs pyramid. Although esteem and self-actualization might not be paramount to your character's survival, they are imperative to fleshing out your protagonist and gaining your reader's empathy. It's essential that you understand your character's goals and motivations in a story, including how they might change, according to author E.M. Welsh. Welsh's writing blog offers several resources for authors to use in order to better understand their characters' motivations in a story. For even more resources and examples to help you determine your character's goals, visit Bang2Write's screenwriting blog post "23 Powerful Examples of Character Motivation" or explore the character motivation worksheet offered on "Lady Writer" Eva Deverell's writing resources website (https://www.eadeverell.com/character-motivation/).

By incorporating your characters' needs into your manuscript, you'll be one step closer to making them feel real to the reader instead of wooden, two-dimensional pawns that exist just to drive your plot. ■

Gayle Trent

The Hero's Journey

WHAT MAKES A GREAT ACTION-ADVENTURE STORY?

Ever popular, the Action-Adventure story is the original hero's journey: a protagonist who must go on a quest to a new world and fight demons—both inner and outer—along the way. With such flexible parameters, the genre is one that often must share the spotlight, whether it crosses with Fantasy and Sci-Fi epics, Thrillers, Mysteries, or another category of fiction. Even Romances have been known to cross over into the Action-Adventure realm from time to time. However, with the popularity of movies like *National Treasure* and books such as Dan Brown's *The Da Vinci Code*, Action-Adventure has made a name for itself over the years all on its own.

As a genre, Action-Adventure fiction is primarily defined by a heroic physical quest where, should our protagonist fail to rise to the challenge, dire consequences await. Typically, the fate of a nation, a species, or an entire universe rests upon the hero's shoulders. In undertaking the quest, our protagonist is not only saving their people but also beginning to understand the true power of their own character.

Readers will correctly assume that the protagonist in an Action-Adventure story will come out a winner, but it's the journey—both physical and emotional—of getting there that will keep readers gripped and turning pages. Let's explore some elements that make for good Action-Adventure stories.

ELEMENTS OF GOOD ACTION-ADVENTURE STORIES

Readers who love the Action-Adventure genre will want specific sequences and tropes from such a story. These include:

A likable hero: The protagonist in an Action-Adventure tale is an ordinary person who's been thrown into an extraordinary situation. This is not someone who expected—or sometimes even wanted—to be a hero, but the situation has demanded they rise to the challenge. The hero must be likable and relatable and often follows a strict moral code, which means they won't take shortcuts or do underhanded things, even when pushed into a corner.

A classic villain: The "bad guy" in an Action-Adventure story can be a villain, a situation, or, oftentimes, both. The antagonist will do everything in their power to prevent the hero from succeeding in their quest, and it's these challenges that both raise the stakes for the other characters and heighten the tension for readers. The villain will typically revel in the hero's misery and often has a master plan of their own, which they can only achieve with the hero's failure. Although the hero is often an ordinary person, the villain is both powerful and motivated.

A quest: The one thing that sets the Action-Adventure story apart from other genres is the quest. Our hero must leave their current physical location and comfort zone and embark on a journey to a new place and time, where the rules are different and the challenges unknown. It is this unfamiliar environment and the uncertainty of the path that keeps readers coming back to Action-Adventure stories. There are a lot of world-building opportunities in Action-Adventure tales, and smart writers will incorporate elements from the new world to create both conflict and tension.

High stakes: It's important to remember that Action-Adventure stories, whether they're novels, short stories, movies, or video games, are often high concept and therefore have high stakes. The consequences of failure are death and destruction on a large scale. On a smaller scale, throughout the narrative, the hero must face personal peril. As the risks get progressively greater, so does the hero's confidence. A ticking-clock scenario is commonly used in Action-Adventure novels.

Action sequences: This is a plot-driven story that must offer plenty of action sequences. The average Action-Adventure film contains nine action sequences, according to the screenwriting resource Ink & Cinema (https://www.inkandcinema.com), and that's the pace you want for your story or novel as well. These action sequences, be they car chases or gun battles, should place the reader in the middle of the action and offer a visceral experience, keeping them on the edges of their seats.

Transformation: Some Action-Adventure protagonists will maintain a neutral character arc and change very little over the course of the story. But for those characters who do change, by the end of the story, the hero who started their journey as an ordinary person will no longer be the same. In these cases, the story will show us the journey and the road that led to the transition, and at the end, there must be a final battle in which readers can clearly recognize that transition, making the journey from ordinary person to hero complete. ■

Natasha Khullar Relph

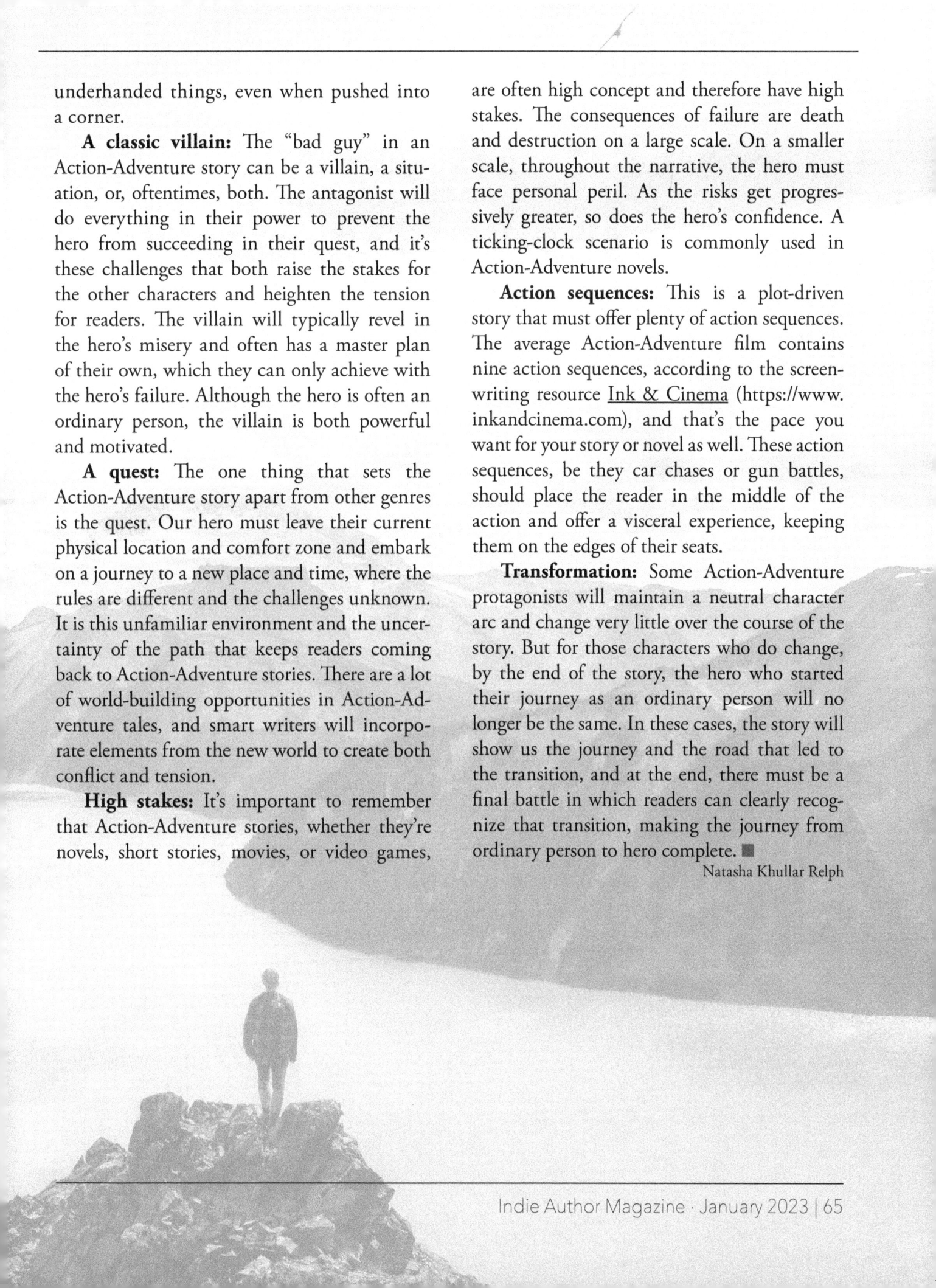

Outline Your Future as a Prosperous Writer

I discovered the beauty of knowing other writers at the Colonists Summit back in 2014. At that conference, two dozen writers came together to talk all things writing and publishing. I was in heaven.

Although I knew about the concept of starving artists, and therefore writers, I'd worked on my overall money consciousness such that by the time I started writing and publishing books, I had the solid expectation I would earn money from them. So I did.

At the conference, I found that about half of the attendees were earning a living from their writing. The other half weren't and shared they didn't believe they could. It inspired me to help them, so I created the Prosperity for Writers course prior to writing the book, *Prosperity for Writers*.

I know every breakthrough in life and work begins with a decision. My big decision when I turned forty was to become a full-time writer. With just two books to my credit at the time, I gave myself five years to turn writing, and books, into my full-time, mega-money-making career.

Here's where outlining comes into play. I want to help you eliminate your money blocks—or at least get started on eliminating them—in this article and

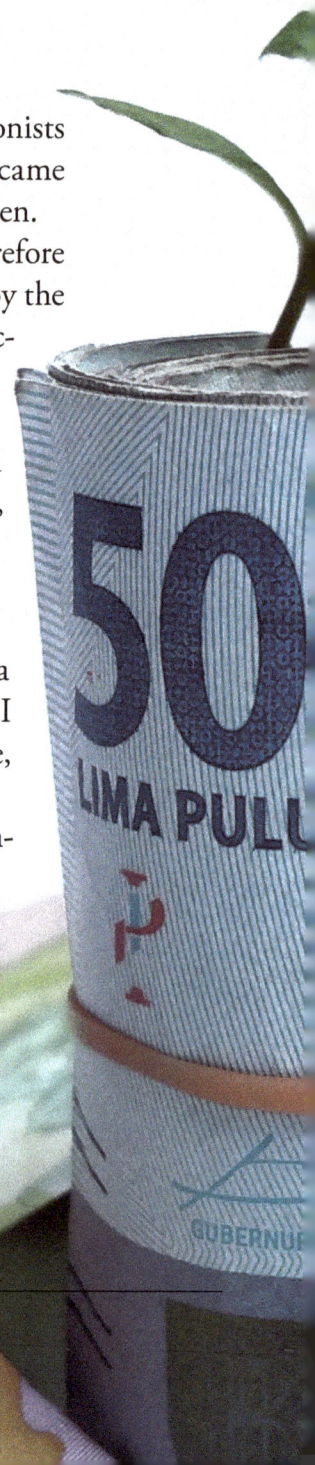

throughout this series. I hope I'm not the first person to tell you that you can earn a living from your writing.

Even if you know this, if you haven't figured out how to grease the wheels, it might surprise you to learn that earning a living from your writing is as much based on your thoughts and beliefs as it is your writing.

Now I'm not suggesting you can be a terrible writer and still make a fortune, though we all probably just brought someone to mind who has. I'm saying you'll write better when your mindset game is tight. I'm here to help you get it right where it needs to be. And we'll start by creating an outline for your future success as a writer, simple, easy, and in writing.

Line One: Make a Decision. Decide what you want, and by when. Draw a line in the sand and decide how you want your writing career to be, when it needs to get there, and how incredible you're going to feel when it does. Dream big; shoot for the stars. What have you got to lose? Hint: Not a thing. Write a line like this: "By the time I'm forty-five, I'm going to be earning a living as a writer, making at least one hundred thousand dollars a year from royalties." If this is too much, too soon, try deciding what just this year will look like by the time you ring in the next new year.

Line Two: Give Yourself Permission to Make Money as a Writer. You might be making a fine living doing something else, or you might have never earned as much as you'd like. Either way, set aside anything you might have assumed was not possible for you and embrace the possibility of an incredible, prosperous future. Write a line to yourself about yourself, such as, "I am a writer. I earn a fantastic living as a writer, writing books about writing for those who want to write better and make money more easily." You might also want to read Jeff Goins' *Real Artists Don't Starve*. His writing is helpful to reinforce your burgeoning beliefs it is perfectly fine to prosper as a writer.

Line Three: Decide Money Is Awesome, You Love Money, and Money Loves You. Stay with me here; this is important. If you have any negative energy or thoughts around money—that it's bad or that having it makes a person bad—you've got to get rid of them. If you don't like something, do you want to be around it? If someone doesn't like you, do you want to be around them? Nope and nope.

If you haven't had money, perhaps it is a challenge to envision you could have it. That, then, would be your first step—begin to imagine you not only have money but also that the money comes from your writing. It might be fiction at first, but I promise, with continued use of your creative imagination, you can turn what is now fiction into nonfiction. If you can't get into the "I love money!" spirit, at least find a way to be neutral about it. You probably didn't fall in love on your first date, so this part may take time. It is worth it, I promise you.

That's it! Put your three statements up where you can see them daily, and if you're feeling extra motivated, say them out loud twice a day. I'm looking forward to hearing what happens next. ∎

Honorée Corder

New Year's Resolutions Every Indie Author Can Set for a Healthier 2023

Not everyone makes a New Year's resolution, but the people who do usually focus on <u>health and wellness</u>. Last year, 23 percent of Americans aimed to live healthier in the new year, making it the most popular resolution in 2022, according to Statista. As an indie author, it's great to concentrate on your 2023 business strategies, but to maintain or exceed your productivity, you might benefit from adding wellness goals as well.

MAKE WELLNESS A PRIORITY

Creating goals to counteract <u>health risks associated with sitting</u> can help protect physical and mental well-being in the long term. According to the Mayo Clinic, extended time sitting and working on a computer can result in:

- eye strain
- Repetitive Strain Injury (<u>RSI</u>)
- tension headaches
- neck, back, and shoulder pain
- weight gain
- high blood pressure

These issues could impair creativity and lead to additional health concerns if not addressed.

PLOT TWIST

Most indie authors have endless to-do lists, so why not make a not-to-do list? Like our characters, what makes us happy or inspires us can change. However, the best-laid writing plans may go astray when virtual tasks take all your time, fill you with negativity, or drain your creative energy.

Most of us don't write a novel overnight. Instead, we write chapter by chapter and can plan to do the same with our health using measurable, achievable wellness goals. Decide what you want to reduce or eliminate, then create specific goals for your physical and mental well-being, such as:

- I won't overschedule; I'll plan specific days or times to keep open.
- I won't overindulge in junk food, alcohol, or negativity.
- I won't sit for more than (#) minutes at a time.
- I won't sleep fewer than (#) hours a night.
- I won't drink more than (#) caffeinated beverages a day.
- I won't spend more than (#) minutes or hours on social media a day.
- I won't forget to celebrate every success.

Remember that habits take time to form or break, so maintain a positive mindset. If you get off track, start fresh. Think of how often you might rewrite a chapter or a sentence until you get it just right. You don't give up on your writing, so don't give up on yourself and your health goals easily. Keep at it, and before long, you'll be well on your way to forming healthy habits that last. ◼

Maureen Bonatch

Resolve to Change Your Mindset

CREATING AN AUTHOR VALUE STATEMENT FOR THE NEW YEAR

Every year, people around the world make grand plans for lifestyle makeovers that are sure to bring them closer to their dreams. Six months in, more than half of the people who make a resolution will have given it up, according to Discover Happy Habits (https://discoverhappyhabits.com/new-years-resolution-statistics/).

Authors in particular sometimes struggle with creating concrete resolutions since so many of the factors of success feel beyond their control.

One solution may be to think bigger. Although the sellers of specialized planners will probably disagree, setting specific, measurable goals and breaking them down into accessible steps isn't always motivating. Even with a clear track to success, it's easy to become overwhelmed or burned out.

Instead, consider taking the macro view by creating a value statement in place of your annual resolution. Value statements express who you already are and can help you focus on what you want while maintaining a positive mindset. They give you a motivating call to action rather than another goal you'll need to motivate yourself to accomplish.

From a practical standpoint, narrowing down what's important for you and your book business to a concise statement of purpose allows for more flexibility in defining your goals. You can change the way you measure success throughout the year, as long as every action you take aligns with your stated values.

Creating a value statement also brings clarity to your author brand and gives you another way to communicate with readers. Consistency in your messaging, from marketing materials to the content of your books, builds confidence in your reading community.

If committing to a New Year's resolution feels daunting, try changing your mindset instead. Create a motivating value statement, and celebrate who you already are.

Ready to get started? Check out how these authors explain their process:

- Marisa Mohi breaks down the difference between a vision, core values, and a mission or purpose, and explains why they should all be part of your writer's vision statement. (https://marisamohi.com/writers-vision-statement)
- Erica Liodice gives you three steps to defining why you write in a 2020 post from Writer Unboxed. (https://writerunboxed.com/2020/06/04/how-and-why-to-create-an-author-mission-statement)
- Cygnet Brown of HubPages explores ways to make sure your mission statement reflects your personality. (https://discover.hubpages.com/literature/mission_statement_writing) 🟧

Jenn Lessmann

'Boon for the Spirits'

VOLUNTEERS BEHIND THIS YEAR'S 20BOOKS VEGAS SAY GIVING THEIR TIME IS ITS OWN REWARD

At the 20Books Vegas 2022 conference, the 6 a.m. volunteer shift buzzes with energy. People from all corners of the world run off in groups to unload swag from vehicles, unpack notebooks, and prepare their stations. I was lucky enough to be among them for my second year, and to capture a rare group photo after 20BooksTo50K® leader and conference organizer Craig Martelle's morning pep talk for the first front desk crew of around thirty people. Another group will replace this first crew after

the check-in rush has subsided, with several of them moving to the hall to guide check-in traffic. The organizers spent a lot of time considering traffic flow and human needs in determining how to create a smooth flow. Considering the military background of the Martelle family, it is unsurprising that it takes on a regimented air. It is part military operation and part family reunion, everyone alternatively reaching for boxes of swag and hugs after a year apart. New volunteers swirl among the love, soaking up the energy and making new friends.

This early Monday morning crew deals with jet lag, a lack of breakfast, and not enough coffee. As the conference moves forward, volunteer energy moves a little slower, either from imbibing a bit much the night before or from exhaustion brought on by learning immersion; coffee becomes more important. Kelly O'Donnell, an LMBPN volunteer, can be found at the front desk assisting Tammy Martelle, Craig Martelle's sister, most of the week with check-ins. Her advice to volunteers: "Get your coffee early. Get your second cup of coffee early." She's quickly proven right. Among the check-in buzz on Monday were whispers of the coffee table being set up and offers to get each other a cup.

Most of us know that the front desk check-in is all-volunteer, but we cannot forget that the AV (Audio Visual) club, hall and room monitors, and even the presenters are donating their time to share their knowledge and be of service to other authors. Each type of volunteer has found their niche—the former flight attendant (me) leans toward check-in while the technologically savvy lean toward the AV club.

There is a great deal of work behind the scenes to create and manage volunteers as well, from deciding where an individual fits to planning for restroom breaks and no-shows. Tammy Martelle donates her time to guide the larger crowd of volunteers, never breaking her smile. Volunteer leadership isn't easy, but she makes it look as if it is.

What is it that drives these humans to donate their time? To find out, I took time between my own volunteer duties at 20Books Vegas to interview some of them.

Many say they have been volunteering since they were children, donating their time as Brownies and Candy Stripers, assisting with trail building, and delivering food to seniors through Meals on Wheels. "I've been volunteering since I was a Big Brother with Big Brothers Big Sisters, in a program for adult men to read to kids in schools, and to help keep boys reading," says Alex Bates, a presenter. Bates also spent time at the 2022 conference offering an introduction to Dungeons & Dragons for newcomers to the game. Volunteering, he says, is a "boon for the spirits. So much of what we do as independent creators is so solitary. It's nice to be around your people."

Volunteering can also be a powerful way to connect with your tribe, says Kat Adele, who designed a writer-focused fabric and sewed an apron to wear for her first time attending 20Books. Adele says she volunteered as a way to meet other writers. She already has volunteered for several years at a local writers' conference, finding that it helps her to "be more aware and present during the conference."

Volunteering gives people a sense of pride, and even owner-ship of the mission of an organization. This mission helps volunteer recruitment and longevity. 20BooksTo50K®, with its strict and hearty vision that "a rising tide lifts all boats," draws volunteers who desire to take part in that mission. The volunteer signup for the 20books Vegas events exceeds the need, highlighting the strength of the mission and the charisma of the leaders. These volunteers do not seek perks, for there are none. However, this year, volunteers were given 20BooksTo50K® bags, a delightful surprise to all. These bags became conversation starters, even among volunteers of different groups. I found myself approached based upon this bag and made connections with volunteers I wouldn't have otherwise met.

"I swing wildly between the introvert/extrovert pendulum," Adele says. "Volunteering initially provides a shield"—a shield that is often helpful for introvert authors visiting an extrovert city like Las Vegas, with nineteen

hundred of their peers in one place. For the introvert writer, even being in a crowded space with writing peers can be overwhelming. Like Adele, during my first year at 20Books, volunteering allowed me to make a few connections before a sea of faces descended upon the conference center. Those connections provided the shield against the unknown. Although I already felt that every attendee was going to be one of "my people," by volunteering, I automatically had people to wave to later, even if our genres were unconnected. The sense of belonging was enhanced by volunteering.

For repeat volunteers, friendships formed previously reinforced the drive to volunteer again. Cristen Jester, in her second year volunteering with 20Books, says that volunteering brings "a sense of ease in seeing familiar faces." Repeat volunteers added to the "well-oiled machine" of the check-in process. The volunteers' bonds grew beyond a polite camaraderie to a family on a mission to help others.

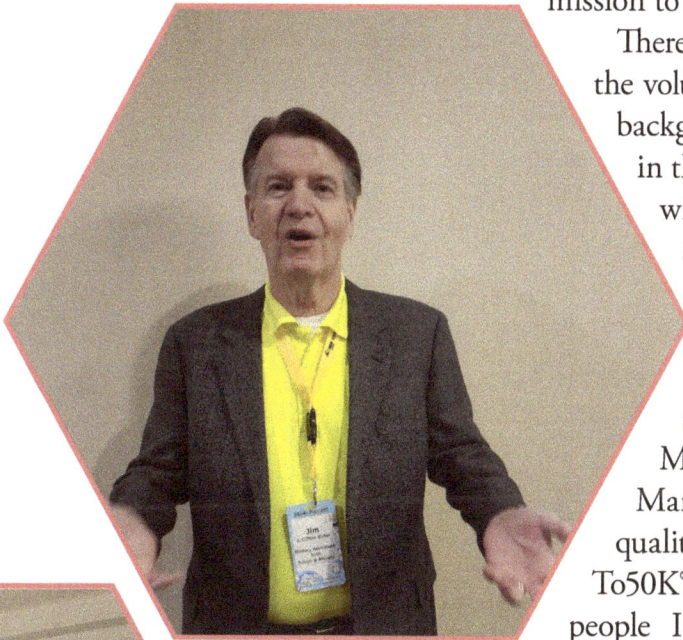

There is a recurring theme among the volunteers: a history of military background either personally or in their family. Military families withstand a great deal of adversity. From tasks that test their souls, to long deployments to eating MREs, military families are resilient, stoic, and most of all, loyal. The Martelles, with their deep Marine connection, carry these qualities over to the 20Books-To50K® family. The majority of people I spoke with had military connections. These connections come through personal service, as active duty, retired, or veterans; often, this connection is through marriage or being born in military hospitals. Overall, this group of volunteers shared the sense of duty they feel to one another and a shared sense of loyalty to their peers. Dale Grantham, one of the spouse volunteers, gives his time during the conference to support his wife. "It gives her a positive outlook," he says. "We were both raised

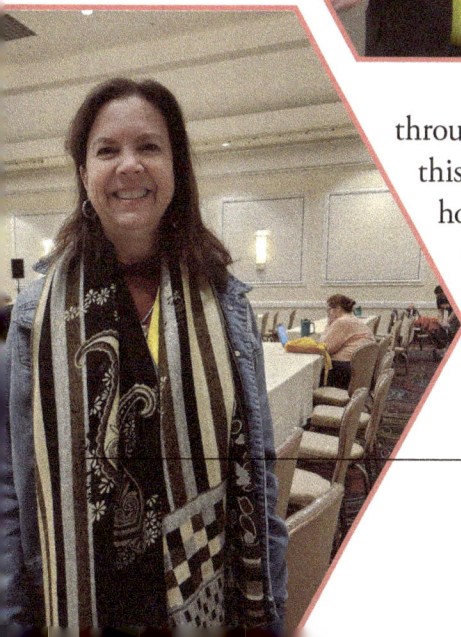

in the military, where everyone was family." A form of ultimate volunteering, those with this military background see volunteering as a responsibility. "I'm not satisfied unless I am participating in some way in some type of service—it feeds my soul," says Terry Wells-Brown, adding that it brings her "a sense of worth" to help others.

Creating a safe and welcoming environment is vital for the success of a conference as large as 20Books Vegas. From keeping conference-crashers out of the conference area to making sure that each attendee feels safe, the hall and room monitors are guided by J. Clifton Slater, a duty he describes as vital. "I coach the room monitors to be a safe harbor. Put introvert writers in a crowded hallway, they panic. They need to know there is always someone to go to." Slater, self-proclaimed "swag hag," lives near Las Vegas and also donates space in his home to the accumulation of the swag for the event, assuring the success of other volunteer groups, like check-in.

Volunteering can have material benefits, from getting badges early to receiving a 20Books tote bag or lunch in a suite for the volunteers. Yet not a single interviewee mentioned these tangible benefits. Deann Powell, who has been volunteering since she was a child, says she volunteers for 20Books as "a chance to give back to the community because it is a lot for Craig and Tammy to put on here."

Volunteering has its costs as well. Audio-Visual volunteers often miss out on networking and sessions they want to attend, room monitors miss out on cookies while they give directions, and presenters miss out on other sessions they would like to attend. Regardless, never a complaint passed anyone's lips. The drive to make a difference was stronger. "This group is all about giving back. Volunteering is a step in the right direction," says second-time volunteer E. W. Barnes. "My ultimate goal is to help authors come to the event and to meet everyone's needs."

Giving back to the author community drives each of these volunteers, but what do the volunteers say is the most important benefit of volunteering for their author community? One word: belonging.

Over the course of the week, the buzz of volunteering turns to networking: business cards collected and social media exchanged.

With glasses raised in cheer at after-hours gatherings, lifelong friendships are made, anthologies plotted, and co-authors corralled. As the conference winds down, volunteers run into each other one last time, exchanging hugs with the promise to see each other at next year's 6 a.m. Monday shift. The conference hall quiets to a hum as bags are packed. A trickle of indie authors and entrepreneurs make their way to their cars or taxis, returning home to recover and reflect.

The volunteers perhaps carry something greater home with them: an extraordinary connection to the message of 20BooksTo50K®, that "a rising tide lifts all boats." Jenn Mitchell, a check-in volunteer, sums up the overall feeling that remains: "This is the one thing in life I get more out of than I put into." ■

Heather Clement Davis

From the Stacks

Courtesy of IndieAuthorTools.com
Got a book you love and want to share with us?
Submit a book at IndieAuthorTools.com

Free Your Time: How Assistants Supercharge Successful Authors

Grace Snoke
https://books2read.com/u/4X2yG1

Author, personal assistant, and *Indie Author Magazine* contributor Grace Snoke comes out swinging with her first nonfiction book for indie authors.

It can be overwhelming to handle all the various tasks and responsibilities that come with being an author. You may find that some of these tasks don't come naturally to you, or that you simply don't have the time or energy to complete them all. In these cases, it may be helpful to consider hiring a virtual assistant to help you manage your workload.

If you're considering hiring a virtual assistant, you may have questions about what tasks you can delegate to them, how to safely share accounts with them, and where to begin the hiring process. This guide aims to answer these questions and provide a helpful starting point for authors who are considering hiring a virtual assistant.

Stop Making Others Rich: How Authors Can Make Bank By Selling Direct

Morgana S. Best
https://books2read.com/u/31DNwW

An author store can be a powerful tool for managing and growing your author business. With the right store, you can upsell, retarget customers, and bundle products in a way that isn't possible through traditional retailers. You can also get paid faster and retain more of your profits, as you won't be subject to the long payment schedules and cuts that retailers often require. Additionally, an author store gives you access to valuable data and analytics about your customer base, helping you to make informed decisions about your business. In this book, you'll learn how to set up and optimize an author store, including tips on which storefront platform to use, how to handle international sales tax, and how to manage change in the industry. Whether you're just starting out or have an existing store, this book can help you take control of your author finances and make the most of your business.

The Anatomy of Genres: How Story Forms Explain the Way the World Works

John Truby

https://books2read.com/u/meKWQE

Genres are not just categories for entertainment choices but rather the most popular and successful stories in the world. John Truby, a writing teacher and author, has written a guide called *The Anatomy of Genres* to help writers understand and utilize the basic elements of storytelling in various genres. Truby explains three key rules for successful genre writing and analyzes a variety of genres, identifying the "beats" or key plot events that define each one. He also shows how these beats can be combined to create unique and effective stories that blend elements of different genres. *The Anatomy of Genres* aims to improve the quality and impact of writers' stories.

Romancing Your Goals

Zoe York

https://books2read.com/u/mK6gjL

Are you a genre fiction writer looking to succeed in your career? In *Romance Your Goals*, *New York Times* and *USA Today* bestselling romance author Zoe York provides a framework for achieving your goals as a writer. This book includes decision-making tools and a discussion on how to progress in your career without necessarily achieving breakout success. York also offers support for knowing when it's time to take your writing career in a new direction. Whether you're just starting out or looking to take your writing to the next level, *Romance Your Goals* is the perfect guide to help you achieve your ideal career as a writer.

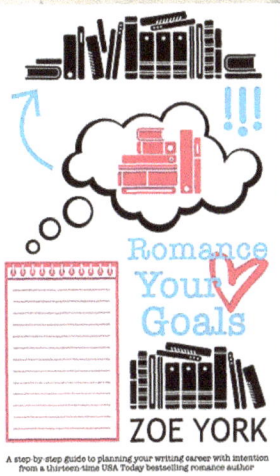

Help! My Facebook Ads Suck

Mal Cooper and Jill Cooper

https://books2read.com/u/bQj850

Publisher's Note: Just prior to the 20BooksTo50K® conference in Las Vegas, Mal Cooper and Jill Cooper held an event, teaching more than fifty authors how to optimize their Facebook ads. In a word, I found it stunning. The examples they showed were clearly structured and easy to understand, and the practical applications for authors of any genre were compelling. Rather than the generic fluff that most Facebook ads training offer, this was specific, timely, and useful. If you're struggling with Facebook ads, this book is a great start. – CH

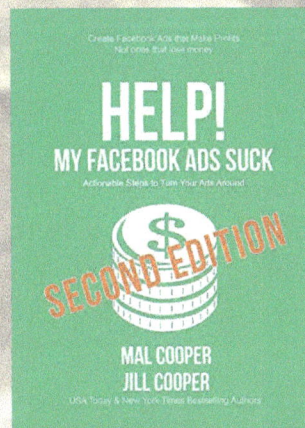

In This Issue

Executive Team

Chelle Honiker, Publisher

As the publisher of Indie Author Magazine, Chelle Honiker brings nearly three decades of startup, technology, training, and executive leadership experience to the role. She's a serial entrepreneur, founding and selling multiple successful companies including a training development company, travel agency, website design and hosting firm, a digital marketing consultancy, and a wedding planning firm. She's organized and curated multiple TEDx events and hired to assist other nonprofit organizations as a fractional executive, including The Travel Institute and The Freelance Association.

As a writer, speaker, and trainer she believes in the power of words and their ability to heal, inspire, incite, and motivate. Her greatest inspiration is her daughters, Kelsea and Cathryn, who tolerate her tendency to run away from home to play with her friends around the world for months at a time. It's said she could run a small country with just the contents of her backpack.

Alice Briggs, Creative Director

As the creative director of Indie Author Magazine, Alice Briggs utilizes her more than three decades of artistic exploration and expression, business startup adventures, and leadership skills. A serial entrepreneur, she has started several successful businesses. She brings her experience in creative direction, magazine layout and design, and graphic design in and outside of the indie author community to her role.

With a masters of science in Occupational Therapy, she has a broad skill set and uses it to assist others in achieving their desired goals. As a writer, teacher, healer, and artist, she loves to see people accomplish all they desire. She's excited to see how IAM will encourage many authors to succeed in whatever way they choose. She hopes to meet many of you in various places around the world once her passport is back in use.

Nicole Schroeder, Editor in Chief

Nicole Schroeder is a storyteller at heart. As the editor in chief of Indie Author Magazine, she brings nearly a decade of journalism and editorial experience to the publication, delighting in any opportunity to tell true stories and help others do the same. She holds a bachelor's degree from the Missouri School of Journalism and minors in English and Spanish. Her previous work includes editorial roles at local publications, and she's helped edit and produce numerous fiction and nonfiction books, including a Holocaust survivor's memoir, alongside independent publishers. Her own creative writing has been published in national literary magazines. When she's not at her writing desk, Nicole is usually in the saddle, cuddling her guinea pigs, or spending time with family. She loves any excuse to talk about Marvel movies and considers National Novel Writing Month its own holiday.

Monthly Columnists

Honorée Corder

Honorée Corder is the author of more than fifty books, an empire builder, and encourager of writers. When she's not writing, she's spoiling her dog and two cats, eating something fabulous her husband made on the grill, working out, or reading. She hopes this article made a positive impact on your life, and if it did, you'll reach out to her via Honoree-Corder.com.

Craig Martelle

High school Valedictorian enlists in the Marine Corps under a guaranteed tank contract. An inauspicious start that was quickly superseded by excelling in language study. Contract waived, a year at the Defense Language Institute to learn Russian and off to keep my ears on the big red machine during the Soviet years. Earned a four-year degree in two years by majoring in Russian Language. My general staff. career included choice side gigs – UAE, Bahrain, Korea, Russia, and Ukraine.

Major Martelle. I retired from the Marines after a couple years at the embassy in Moscow working arms control issues.

Department of Homeland Security then law school next. I was working for a high-end consulting firm performing business diagnostics, business law, and leadership coaching. For the money they paid me, I was good with that. Just until I wasn't. Then I started writing.

Contributors

Maureen Bonatch

Maureen Bonatch MSN, RN, is a fiction author and freelance healthcare writer. Her experience as a fiction author helps her create engaging and creative content as she authors numerous healthcare articles and online educational content. Maureen writes cozy paranormal mysteries as M.L. Bonatch and urban fantasy, paranormal romance, and other genres as Maureen Bonatch.

When Maureen's not doing the bidding of a feisty Shih Tzu, she's a mom to twin daughters, exploring the beautiful woods of PA with her hubby and dancing as much as possible. She believes in pairing music with every mood, that laughter is contagious, and caffeine and wine are essential for survival. She is the owner of MaureenBonatch.com and CharmedType.com.

Heather Clement Davis

Heather Clement Davis holds twenty-six years' experience in museums, archaeology, art, art therapy, creative writing, and nonprofit management. She holds enough graduate work to make a Ph.D. cry as her neurodivergent brain is hooked on learning everything. Her paintings and pottery are in galleries and collections worldwide and her poetry, nonfiction and fiction has found its way to literary journals around the U.S. When not writing or making art, Heather can be found playing Magic the Gathering, Dungeons and Dragons, or watching Star Trek with her family.

Laurel Decher

There might be no frigate like a book, but publishing can feel like a voyage on the H.M.S. Surprise. There's always a twist and there's never a moment to lose.

Laurel's mission is to help you make the most of today's opportunities. She's a strategic problem-solver, tool collector, and co-inventor of the "you never know" theory of publishing.

As an epidemiologist, she studied factors that help babies and toddlers thrive. Now she writes books for children ages nine to twelve about finding more magic in life. She's a member of the Society for Children's Book Writers and Illustrators (SCBWI), has various advanced degrees, and a tendency to smuggle vegetables into storylines.

Gill Fernley

Gill Fernley writes fiction in several genres under different pen names, but what all of them have in common is humour and romance, because she can't resist a happy ending or a good laugh. She's also a freelance content writer and has been running her own business since 2013. Before that, she was a technical author and documentation manager for an engineering company and can describe to you more than you'd ever wish to know about airflow and filtration in downflow booths. Still awake? Wow, that's a first! Anyway, that experience taught her how to explain complex things in straightforward language and she hopes it will come in handy for writing articles for IAM. Outside of writing, she's a cake decorator, expert shoe hoarder, and is fluent in English, dry humour and procrastibaking.

Belinda Griffin

Belinda K Griffin is a Book Marketing Coach and Author Publicity Expert at SmartAuthorsLab.com. She helps authors of all kinds launch and market their books with impact, so they can grow a thriving community of engaged readers and sell more books. Growing a loyal readership and securing publicity through authentic relationship building and outreach is at the heart of everything she teaches.

Audrey Hughey

Audrey Hughey designs planners, writes fiction, and works diligently to help her fellow authors. Although she currently writes horror and thrillers, she's as eclectic in her writing tastes as in her reading. When she's not submerged in the worlds of fiction and nonfiction, she's caring for her family, enjoying nature, or finding more ways to bring a little more light into the world.

Natasha Khullar Relph

Natasha Khullar Relph is an award-winning journalist, an indie author, and the founder of The Wordling, a weekly business newsletter for writers that delivers the latest in writing and publishing trends and opportunities. Natasha has helped thousands of writers break into dream publications, create six-figure incomes, and launch successful book campaigns. Sign up to The Wordling to get free copies of her best-selling books as well as resources and trainings on how to write and sell more. https://www.thewordling.com

Jenn Lessmann

Jenn Lessmann is the author of three stories published on Amazon's Kindle Vella, two unpublished novels, and a blog that tests Pinterest hacks in the real world (where supplies are sometimes limited, and all projects are overseen by children with digital attention spans). A former barista, stage manager, and high school English teacher with advanced degrees from impressive colleges, she continues to drink excessive amounts of caffeine, stay up later than is absolutely necessary, and read three or four books at a time. She loves lists and the rule of three. Irony too. Jenn is currently studying witchcraft and the craft of writing, and giggling internally whenever they intersect. She writes snarky (not spicy) paranormal fantasy for new adults whenever her dog will allow it.

Megan Linski-Fox

Megan Linski lives in Michigan. She is a USA TODAY Bestselling Author and the author of more than fifty novels. She has over fifteen years of experience writing books alongside working as a journalist and editor. She graduated from the University of Iowa, where she studied Creative Writing.

Megan advocates for the rights of the disabled, and is an activist for mental health awareness. She co-writes the Hidden Legends Universe with Alicia Rades. She also writes under the pen name of Natalie Erin for the Creatures of the Lands series, co-authored by Krisen Lison.

Eryka Parker

Eryka Parker is a book coach, an award-winning developmental editor, and writing instructor. As a women's contemporary author under the pen name Zariah L. Banks, she creates emotional intimacy novels that prove that everyone deserves to feel seen, appreciated, and loved. She lives in Northeast Ohio with her husband and two children and is currently working on her third novel.

Robyn Sarty

Robyn Sarty brings over a decade of experience as an editor and proofreader to Indie Author Magazine. She is the author of two novels and several short stories, and manages her own publishing company. She loves helping other authors with their books and can often be found nerding out over story elements with her friends. She spent five years as a project coordinator for an international engineering firm, and now uses those skills to chase writers instead of engineers and hopes it will be good training for her first marathon. Growing up as a third culture kid, books were the one constant in her life, and as such, Robyn believes that books are portals to the magic that lies within, and authors are wielders of that magic. She also admits to being a staunch, loyal, and unabashed supporter of the Oxford comma.

Gayle Trent

Gayle Leeson is a USA TODAY best-selling, award-winning author who writes multiple cozy mystery series and a portal fantasy series under the pen name

G. Leeson. Gayle has also written as Amanda Lee (the embroidery mystery series) and as Gayle Trent. Visit her online at gayleleeson.com.

Terry Wells-Brown

Terry Wells-Brown lives in the lush California Zinfandel wine country with the love of her life; Don, and their two rescue pups; Jake and Buster. Terry is the author of the romantic suspense series Women of Wine Country, the contemporary fantasy series Earth Magic, and the international collaboration; Sisters of Sin. She is also the feature writer for Best Version Media community magazine; Woodbridge and West Lodi. Besides reading and writing, she devotes her time to her family, tribe, and her small community. During Halloween, Terry enjoys dancing as one of the Witches of Wine Country, and a couple of months later trades in the pointy hat for a red dress where she can be found impersonating Mrs. Claus.

Ready to level up your indie author career?

Trick question. Of course you are.

*INDIE
^Author Tools

Get Your Friday Five Newsletter and find your next favorite tool here.

https://writelink.to/iat

Join the Facebook group here.

https://writelink.to/iatfb